MW01148431

THE NUCLEAR FAMILY

核家族

THE NUCLEAR FAMILY

Ari Beser

Printed in the United States of America
First Printing, 2015

ISBN: 1511482664
ISBN 13: 9781511482660

For the lost souls, above and below
the mushroom clouds.

CONTENTS

HIROSHIMA

BEFORE
                                AFTER

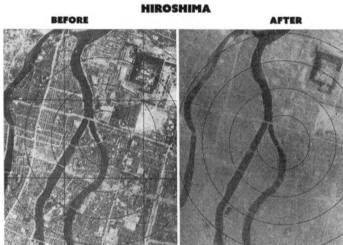

NAGASAKI

BEFORE
                                AFTER

PREFACE

Truth is a malleable concept, yet remains the most valued of virtues. In 2010, in order to uphold the truth, I started discussing the atomic bombs as they related to my family. A book I'll leave nameless was under scrutiny because a person lied about the American perspective depicted in its pages. The author redacted, but the incident left me reeling to tell the true story that connected both sides of the atomic bomb to my family. I wrote a newspaper article for the 65th anniversary of Hiroshima and Nagasaki. It snowballed into a research grant that I won on March 10, 2011 which was already March 11th in Japan. That night distaster struck. As the news unfolded of what would become the Great East Japan Earthquake, Tsunami and Nuclear Disaster, I quickly decided not to give up my plans. I was dedicated to this book. I was dedicated to truth.

How *can* we define truth, especially when it comes to history? Every country has their own truth for every chapter in history. Take Pearl Harbor, for example. What is the truth behind Pearl Harbor?

From one point of view, you see your culture and way of life threatened by a foreign influence largely interested in its own economic gain. You fight that influence off regionally and try to establish your own hegemony, but even more world powers get involved and try to exert their own dominance. Suddenly, one last powerful nation attempts to cut off your energy supply. You could stop fighting altogether, or you could surprise everyone with an attack. On December 8, 1941, this was the frame in which Tokyo viewed its options.

Of course, Americans know a different truth, and because of different time zones, December 7 is the day that will live in infamy. Pearl Harbor was a vicious attack that led to a war Americans didn't want to wage. The Japanese were ruthless warriors who vowed to fight to their last man. They treated prisoners of war like slaves and showed no signs of giving up, even when it was believed they were all but sure to be defeated.

In response to the enslaught that followed Pearl Harbor, the US military took planes that they could have flown at thirty-two thousand feet down to ten thousand and rained firebombs on Japan's wooden cities. The deaths of millions of Japanese soldiers and civilians followed. Endless passions surround World War II. Men and women on both sides will always rally behind their country in the Great War that showed the extent of man's inhumanity.

Americans and Japanese alike may never agree on the history. But the truth to each of them will always remain the same.

The stories in this book are human voices. I have kept these words accurate to how they were told to me or in the case of my grandfather, how they were written. These elderly survivors who asked me to tell their stories, recounted horrific events from nearly seventy years before. In some cases, like in the instance of my grandfather, I was digging through accounts that were twenty-five years outdated, but they were still his opinions nonetheless. In other cases, details were missing, and some people were no longer alive for me to interview. In those cases in which I could not ask people directly, I researched their testimonies and found other sources with which they shared their experiences. I've listed those sources in my Works Cited.

My grandfather carefully researched his own self-published memoir. He felt the need to leave behind a record, a memory of the atomic attacks as a warning to future generations. Any details you read from his chapters come from his own personal archive of information. At times, I felt that some of what he left wasn't enough. When I didn't have enough from the official texts, I talked to my father and my uncles, and we inferred what happened specifically in regard to the Beser family stories. Like many of the Jewish faith, our family's is an oral history.

The people whom I interviewed were not poets nor were they famous writers. They were ordinary people with no exceptional understanding of history, politics, or global nuclear affairs. The bomb was dropped by young men, eager scientists, war-weary pilots, and on top of children and mothers, tramcar drivers, and anyone else who had just started their day in Hiroshima or Nagasaki. All of a sudden, there was a flash of light, and the portal to hell that was the first uranuium and plutonium bombs to be used on people opened up. If you survived it, how would *you* be able to describe what happened next?

It could have ended in Hiroshima and Nagasaki, but those cities were just the beginning. At one point, the Americans and the Soviets were MAD enough to produce sixty thousand nuclear weapons. As of 2015, nine countries have detonated thousands of bombs that have released their radiation into the ground, or the atmosphere, or the water and have permanently altered the course of human history. I don't have the life experience of a survivor of a nuclear attack. I simply wanted to give a voice to the people who do.

* * *

FOREWORD

CLIFTON TRUMAN DANIEL

I met Ari Beser in August 2012 in Hiroshima. Both of us were in Japan as guests of the family of Sadako Sasaki to attend ceremonies marking the sixty-seventh anniversary of the atomic bombings of Hiroshima and Nagasaki.

My grandfather, US President Harry S. Truman, ordered those bombings. Ari's grandfather, Lt. Jacob Beser, was the only American serviceman to fly on both airplanes.

Sadako was two when the bomb destroyed her home in Hiroshima. She survived largely unscathed but was diagnosed with radiation-induced leukemia nine years later. In an effort to help with her treatment, she followed a Japanese tradition that holds if you fold one thousand origami paper cranes, you are granted a wish, health, or a long life. The legend varies. She folded fifteen hundred cranes but died from the leukemia in October 1955.

Masahiro Sasaki, Sadako's older brother, and his son Yuji have been donating the last of those cranes to memorials around the world as gestures of peace and healing. When I met them in 2010, they were giving one to the 9/11 Memorial in New York. Two years later, they gave another to the USS *Arizona* Memorial in Pearl Harbor.

Both Ari and I have held the last crane Sadako folded before she died.

In addition to the ceremonies in Hiroshima and Nagasaki, Ari, my family, and I heard testimony from more than two-dozen survivors. This was the first time I had been to Japan and the first time I heard directly what it had been like to survive the bombings. Ari was a step ahead of me. He was in Japan the year before, already working on his book. In 2011, he volunteered to help clean up in the wake of the tsunami and earthquake that had devastated coastal towns and caused the meltdown at the nuclear plant in Fukushima.

At the Peace Memorial Ceremony in Nagasaki, Ari showed up in a T-shirt advertising the region.

"I could have dressed nicely," he said. "But if the cameras are here, I want to send a message."

Ari's been trying to do that ever since. When my son Wesley and I returned in the summer of 2013 to record survivor testimony for the Truman Presidential Library, Ari was already there, interning at the Hiroshima Peace Memorial Museum.

That September, I joined Peace Boat, a Japanese non-profit offering education on peace, disarmament, and environmental stewardship during three annual global voyages. Ari was already on the boat, having gone straight there from Hiroshima in July. When I arrived at port in Montego Bay, Jamaica, I met Ari's father, Eric. His son had been gone for a year, and Eric wanted to spend just half a day with him before he took off again. Jamaica was as close as Peace Boat was going to get to the United States.

The minute Ari stepped off Peace Boat, he signed up to live and work in Rwanda. At a nonprofit boarding school called Agahozo Shalom Youth Village, he ran the media lab.

He's home now, but who knows for how long. Ari's restless. He keeps searching. Whether he's in Hiroshima or on Peace Boat or in Rwanda, he's looking for ways to help, and he's looking for answers. The nice Jewish boy from Baltimore has become a monk of sorts, wandering the earth in blue jeans and boat shoes.

He carries this manuscript with him, thinking about the stories of Hiroshima and Nagasaki, writing about what they mean to him and to the rest of us. All the survivors asked of us was that we listen and remember. Ari has gone a step further and made them part of himself—let them drive him to try to do better for the survivors, for himself, and for us all.

*   *   *

BEFORE IT'S TOO LATE

2011

I'm in Japan on a research grant to write a book I do not have permission to write, I tapped into my iPhone while gliding three hundred miles per hour on a bullet train to the most important dinner of my life. My host, Mei, would either allow me to write this book, or she would not. *If she says yes, I have to start writing. If she says no, I have to start over.*

Many people know that my grandfather was on the airplanes that dropped the atomic bombs on Hiroshima and Nagasaki. Few people, however, know that my family has a connection to someone who was underneath the mushroom cloud.

*   *   *

Ten years after the atomic bombs were dropped over Hiroshima, Shigeko Niimoto walked past a church and heard a beautiful song coming from inside. A Buddhist, Shigeko didn't know much about Christianity, but she was enchanted by the melody. She entered the church and met Rev. Kiyoshi Tanimoto. This chance meeting was the beginning of a support group of young women who would eventually be known as the Hiroshima Maidens.

Tanimoto became somewhat famous in America after the publication of John Hersey's *Hiroshima*, which detailed his and five other's survival. Author Pearl S. Buck and editor Norman Cousins partnered with the reverend to bring twenty-five young female survivors from Hiroshima to America for reconstructive surgery.

When Maiden J., as I will call her in this book, was 23, she heard about this initiative. She had already undergone eleven mostly unsuccessful surgeries to remove the thick keloid scars that streaked her face and neck. The atomic bombs had taken away her chance of a normal life, but she was determined to take it back.

Many of the women in Tanimoto's support group— and this was true for many atomic-bomb survivors, including Maiden J—wore masks when facing the public in Japan. The thermal flash of the nuclear reaction burned the girls in whatever positions they had been in ten years ago. Maiden J. had been pointing at a plane at the time and couldn't properly use her arm for ten years. When the girls departed for the United States, one by one, they began to take off their masks, and although they were weeks away from the first operations, their healing had begun.

For a brief moment, the Hiroshima Maidens held the American spotlight. The maidens appeared on television shows like *This Is Your Life* and were interviewed on the radio and by various newspapers.

On one particular day, a *Baltimore Sun* truck driver saw Maiden J.'s smiling face on the cover of a newspaper he was delivering. He looked into her story and was charmed. He wrote to her, visited her in the hospital, and proposed to her multiple times. Each time, Maiden J. told him that she was flattered, but she didn't want the rest of the maidens to receive backlash. She could never express her true gratitude for being brought to America and would have felt terrible if she caused a controversy.

After a year and a half of surgeries, Maiden J. returned to Japan. The doctors were able to grow new skin from her abdomen and graft it onto her face, and while she never looked the same as she did before the bombing, her appearance had improved remarkably. In letters, Maiden J. and her Baltimore suitor continued a conversation that lasted ten years, until he finally proposed one last time. By then, she had fulfilled her academic and professional dreams, but she had never found love. Maiden J.'s family thought it was a bad idea for her to move to a foreign country. She disagreed. She defied her family's advice and followed her heart to America.

Maiden J. had some trouble adjusting to life in America. She knew very little English, and she practiced on her own before she sought work in the field of dressmaking. In

1966, she got a job at the Hecht Company in Baltimore City. She worked in the alteration department alongside a motley crew of international coworkers her new boss, Mr. Cohen, fondly called the UN. At Christmas, the members of the UN would bring in dishes from their home countries. There would be German strudel, Polish pierogi, and Jewish deli. No doubt Maiden J. was able to offer her own traditional delicacy.

Occasionally, customers would ask her about her scars. She would continue her work and calmly tell them her story. Usually, they would apologize to her for what she went through, and that would be it. If a child asked, she would say, "When I was your age, I got burned because I didn't listen to my mommy, so you will listen to your mommy, won't you?"

One day in 1971, Mr. Cohen was noticeably absent. Arriving about an hour later than everyone else, he effervescently waltzed in and gathered everyone's attention. "I'd like to announce that Kay"—his daughter—"is engaged!"

Everyone cheered and offered their congratulations. Maiden J. loved Mr. Cohen's family, especially his two daughters. One of the women in the group asked, "Who's the lucky guy?"

Mr. Cohen replied, "Eric Beser from Pikesville."

The name Beser sent a chill down Maiden J.'s spine. There was only one Beser Family in Baltimore, Maryland. Jacob Beser, she remembered, Eric's father, was on the planes that dropped the atomic bomb on *her*. Every year, the *Baltimore Sun* tried to get "the two Baltimoreans who were there" together for a photo to accompany the article about each of them. Every year, she declined. She wanted nothing to do with him. He was not apologetic about what he had helped do. She didn't go to Kay's wedding; she never wanted to face him. If he walked into their store, she left her position. She remained friends with Mr. Cohen and his side of his growing family, but she never wanted to meet Jacob Beser.

On November 17, 1982, Mr. Cohen fell asleep and never woke up. The doctors said his heart gave out. It was the anniversary of his infant son's death, so it wasn't hard to see why. Everyone who knew him felt shock and grief. When I asked my mother if Maiden J. had attended his funeral, she couldn't remember. It was one of the worst days of her life. My father insists Maiden J. sat behind my mother and my Bubby. If Jacob Beser was there, too, which he should have been, it would have been the only time that Maiden J. and the former crewman were in the same room together. It didn't count. Nothing counted that day except for Mr. Cohen. My grandfather.

The following year, Maiden J. and her husband moved to Japan. With the Baltimore Colts gone in the night, her husband had to suffer only the loss of Orioles games at Memorial Stadium. His wife was happy to be home, so he was happy, too. He taught her nieces English and tried, albeit unsuccessfully, to learn Japanese. For a time, the move worked out, but eventually, he started to miss the creature comforts Baltimore had to offer. The seafood of Japan was amazing, but so were G & M's crab cakes. The pair tried moving back stateside one more time. Before their twenty-fifth anniversary, Maiden J.'s husband underwent surgery and died on the operating table. For the last time, she moved back to Japan.

Every few years, Maiden J. visited Baltimore to see my mother's family, her friends from the UN, and her husband's family. I met her on one such visit when I was eight years old. I admitted, "I can't believe that Grandpa was friends with a survivor and Pop Pop dropped the bomb on her." My mother put a rest to it and nearly regretted bringing me to meet her father's friend. She had thought it would be a good idea to bring me because Maiden J. brought her niece with her, a young adult named Mei. It was a friendly encounter and my first with anyone from Japan. Before we left, they extended an open invitation to my family to come visit them.

"Oh my God, Mom, can we go?" I begged instantly.

"Sure, Ari, when you can pay for it," my mother said with a laugh.

The last contact we had with the Maiden's family was a letter informing us she had passed away. The letter's address was thirteen years outdated by 2011. With no way of getting in touch with her family to ask for permission to write this book and after a receiving the research grant after college, I was determined to write a book about people on both sides of the bomb. All my family had was Maiden

J.'s published autobiography, written in Japanese, as source material. I had no way of contacting her family. I wanted to know what happened to her, so I enlisted the help of a Japanese friend of mine to translate Maiden J.'s autobiography. I had written an op-ed about my family's connection to both sides of the bomb in 2010, and the Japanese media had found out. I had hoped to be able to reach Mei by doing an interview with them. The idea worked too well.

A representative from Maiden J.'s family e-mailed me, but she told me to immediately stop translating her book. They were not pleased that I had started a book without asking for permission. Mei, a grown woman with her own family by then, did remember me as a child but said, "If *anything* is to proceed, we need to talk in person. Please let us know when you can make it here. Now I live in Osaka with my husband and family, but you are welcome."

* * *

I downed two small vending machine cans of coffee and a bottle of an electrolyte drink called Pocari Sweat that tastes way better than its name suggests. I was in a battle against my jet lag on day two of a month-long trip. My eyes were glued on the Japanese scenery jettisoning past. The sun sank just above the mountainous horizon, hitting an angle that ignited the sky into a wild mix of orange, red, and gold rays. Around me, people's noses were stuck in their manga comic books, or their thumbs twittered on their smartphones. Surrounded by the beauty of the Japanese landscape, my eyes were fixed to the endless mountains, rice paddies, and black-tiled homes that stretched as far as the eye could see. All of the daily commuters in the train with me were numb to the beautiful scene unfolding as the bullet train sped on. It was, no doubt, a typical view for everyone else but me.

No matter how dark the stories get, never grow numb to the beauty of Japan, I thought as the last rays of light sank behind the mountains.

My train car was void of gaijin, as the Japanese call foreigners, slang for *gaikokujin*, which literally means "foreign country person." The plane ride over had whole empty rows. Customs, too, had open lines, with security agents eagerly awaiting the arrival of no one. Five months had passed since the nuclear accident in Fukushima, and people were still afraid of Japan, but I never questioned it.

Shin-Osaka was packed, but again, not with tourists. It was rush hour—human rush hour. Like highways, the hallways were under construction, presumably being widened to accommodate traffic. At first, I bumped into people, only then realizing I had been conditioned to walk on the right side. I noticed a natural ebb and flow to the Japanese way of maneuvering in a crowd. With few tourists, it was visible. Like on the streets, the human traffic moved along the left side of the passage and wound around the construction mess with ease. I figured it out quickly enough and could whip through the lines of businesspeople so efficiently, a New Yorker would have approved.

I found a quiet waiting room, pulled out my rent-a-phone, and called Mei.

A woman's voice answered. "Moshi moshi! Ari-kun?"

"Mei-san!" My loud American way of speaking into the phone earned me horrified glares from elder bystanders sitting nearby. *Is this rude?* I thought. I moved outside to the noisy hall.

"I am pulling into the station now, but the traffic is very bad. Please, if you can, meet me in front of the station at the central exit. I am in a Toyota minivan."

You have no idea what she looks like. How are you going to find her? "Sounds good," I said. "See you in front of the station!" I realized that spotting a Toyota minivan in the arrivals lane during rush hour at Osaka's main train station would be like trying to find the Jewish guy with brown hair in New York City. To my advantage, I stood at an even six feet, which in Japan was as good as spotting a Jewish guy in rural Rwanda.

After ten minutes of pacing and people-watching, I noticed a Toyota minivan gravitating toward me. The driver's eyes caught mine in a recognizing gaze. Unsure whether it was the right car, I mouthed her name, "Mei-san?"

She nodded and questioned back, "Ari-kun?" before I jumped in the backseat, where two children were already seated. The boy, at about two, energetically squirmed in his car seat, trying to break free, and the girl, who had recently turned seven, was calmer but too nervous to look me in the eye. The highways through Osaka were as thrilling as the bullet train. One highway literally went through a building.

When we arrived at Mei's house, after all of these years, a bow did not fully express my feelings upon seeing her, so I embraced her in a spontaneous hug. I let go immediately, realizing my faux pas. Surprisingly, it didn't catch her off guard. She laughed it off and said, "We do not hug in Japan. Some never have, but I remember Americans do. You should give one to my mother-in-law one when she finishes cooking dinner. It will be funny."

Mei-san, the ever-gracious Japanese host, immediately served iced oolong tea, along with chewy mochi rice cake covered in sweet red bean paste, to wipe off the summer heat. The children played with the new toys my mother had bought for them as souvenirs from America. They were blissfully unaware of what Mei and I were about to discuss.

"Ari-kun," she said, her eyes narrowing, "what is your plan for being here in Japan?"

"Forgive me if I am forward," I said a bit nervously. "I want to write a book about my grandfather and your aunt—a book about both sides of the atomic bombs." Mei twitched at the words, but I kept talking. "I know how important and—"

"And sensitive," she interjected.

"Yes! Extremely sensitive!" I agreed.

"I think that it is strange, yes. It is a very strange…what is the word?" She muttered "guzen" to the translator app on her phone.

"Coincidence?" I guessed.

"Yes, it is a very strange coincidence," she said, "but I am sorry. The answer is no. My grandmother wants to give my aunt's—er, her daughter's—story to my best friend. She is fluent in both English and Japanese and will do a beautiful job with it. I talk about my aunt and the atomic bombs to only my children. It's a very small action, but this is my way. I am thinking it is important." She looked at her young children, who were blissfully unaware of our heavy conversation.

She continued, saying, "You know, I still have the Raggedy Ann doll your mother sewed for me and my sister when we came as children." She motioned to her daughter and said something in Japanese. Moments later, her daughter came in with the same Raggedy Ann doll that had sat in my living room. "We *can* still be your friends. Seeing you here brings back many good memories but also brings to light many bad ones, too. I can't help you understand those. You need to meet hibakusha in order to understand what happened underneath the mushroom cloud. You need to meet many. Hibakusha are so old now, and we are losing them every day. You have to hear it directly from them before it is too late."

* * *

2

KEIKO OGURA, EIGHT YEARS OLD

Robert Jungk, the first writer to publish a book about the Manhattan Project, was working on his next piece, Children of the Ashes. *He needed his friend Kaoru Ogura, the former director of the Peace Memorial Museum and the first fluent English speaker to run it. Unfortunately for Robert, and for everyone who knew Kaoru, he had passed away. Robert was on his way to Hiroshima, and he needed a coordinator. He knew of only one other person who could help him. Devastated by her loss, Kaoru's wife, Keiko, had become a recluse. Keiko had been teaching herself English when her husband passed away unexpectedly. Robert called her and forcefully persuaded her out of her depression to coordinate his trip in Hiroshima. Since then, Mrs. Keiko Ogura has made it her goal to help foreign visitors hear the stories of the survivors. One day, the grandson of a Jacob Beser arrived in Hiroshima. With the help of Hiroshima's Peace Memorial Museum, we were connected. She agreed to meet with me and tell me her story. We've been friends ever since. She admitted to me one day that she helped me "not because of your grandfather, but because you're American. I would help any American who wanted to understand what happened here in Hiroshima."*

When I was in the second grade, my family lived in the center of the city. When the war broke out, Father didn't ship out. He was too slim. His weight was too low. He was a D-grade soldier, but he was important for the neighborhood.

A year before Hiroshima was destroyed, we moved out to the farmland. My father moved my mother, grandmother, four brothers, younger sister, and me from the center of the city to the outskirts in the northern area, 2.4 kilometers from the city center and the future target of the atomic bomb.

Father had heard a rumor that the big factories, like Mitsubishi, would still be allowed to operate, but all small companies like his would be ordered to close. He decided to spend all night and day using all of his materials to produce grinding stones, his trade. One week later, the order came, shutting down small companies from production. They would be allowed to sell off their merchandise, but production had to cease. Father had all of the grinding stones ready and was allowed to sell them. Hiroshima was a military town, and they were not hard to offload.

He made a huge profit, and we were able to move our whole family of six children to Ushita.

"Why are we moving here? I don't like that name," I complained. *Ushi* means cow, and *ta* means fields.

"We're going to have a nice big house with our own land, and we won't be a target anymore," he reassured.

My eleven-year-old brother was in the fifth grade and had been evacuated with other schoolchildren his age to a temple in the mountain area. However, because I was so young, I had to stay home with my parents.

My thirteen-year-old brother was in his second year of junior high and had been mobilized with the rest of his classmates to remove the debris created by the building demolition project. In case of attack, the government was widening the roads to make for safer escape routes.

On August 6, 1945, I was supposed to go to school like all of my other classmates. But early in the morning, my father said to me, "Keiko, you shouldn't go to school today."

I asked, "Why? The air-raid warning has cleared already, so we will not have any attacks today!"

My father said, "No. I have a feeling that something might happen at your school."

I was shocked and in an ill temper. I ran outside to the road and stood alone under the cloudless blue sky. What could go wrong?

Instead of going to school, I went outside to play with my brother. Suddenly, a brilliant flash burned from the center of the city, and everything around me caught fire. I could feel its heat. The small hill behind our neighborhood started to burn from the flash. There was a giant gust of air, like a typhoon, only stronger. I was thrown in a blast of dust and sand—roof tile, doors, and me. I hit the pavement. Strangely, I couldn't hear anything, and in silence, I lost consciousness.

I woke up in darkness and heard one of my brothers crying out. By and by, I could make out the house, at first in pitch dark but getting lighter. The thatch houses started to burn, and then I saw it. Everything was burning, even the living trees. I was so scared. My father told me not to look directly at the city center, but I was an eight-year-old child; I wanted to see.

Everything in my house was smashed and scattered. The ceiling and roof tiles had blown away. Hundreds of shattered pieces of window glass splintered the walls and pillars. No one could imagine what had happened. Like other neighbors, we thought that our small town had been chosen as a target of an air raid.

Why our little cow town?

"Why such a direct hit?" We were at a loss for words, not knowing what to do next, and we feared the next attack. I rushed to get into our family's shelter.

Soon, the black rain started to fall, but I don't know exactly when. Maybe soon after the bombing—I found that my blouse had dark spots on it. They were sticky, charcoal-colored spots. The rain leaked into our destroyed home and left gray chalk stripes on all the walls.

Later, my thirteen-year-old brother, who had been working as one of the mobilized students, came home. He had been in the field north of Hiroshima JR (Japan Railway) station, looking up at the B-29 bomber as the tiny dot that turned out to be the atomic bomb was released from the aircraft. He had realized an explosive had just dropped.

When my mother saw him walking within shouting distance, she yelled to him, "We are unlucky! A bomb was dropped on us. You are lucky being away from this town."

My brother answered, "Mom, what are you talking about? The whole city is completely destroyed. I saw the city and the huge cloud from the top of the hill on the way back home."

He was so astonished by what had happened to Hiroshima that he didn't notice the burns on his face and arms. His school uniform and cap were tattered and torn. Hearing my brother's story, I cautiously walked out of the gate of the house. I wanted to climb up the stone steps leading to the shrine on the hill. I was a curious little girl, and I wanted to see what was happening in the city. The roads were full of debris and pieces of roof tiles. It was hard to find the way to walk. Then, all of a sudden, I encountered rows of burned and injured people fleeing on the road. Their clothes, and skin were mangled and burned to tatters.

A long, wordless line of victims slowly passed by me like ghosts, bleeding all over, skin peeling off and hanging from the tips of their fingers. Most of them were soldiers and high-school students. Maybe they were fleeing from the central part of the city. Their burned hair smelled bad. Some of their faces and lips were swollen. Some were showing their internal organs. Some were squatting. Some were lying down. Some were already dead on the road and stone steps.

I found out later that the shrine area I was trying to reach had been designated as a relief station for refugees. That was the reason for the long lines of survivors everywhere near my house.

Relatives, friends, neighbors, and strangers gathered at my partially destroyed house, full of the dying. The only thing I could do was give a tomato from our garden to a dying soldier.

My house reeked of blood, puss, dirt, burned hair, and filth.

I went outside, and as I was walking on the road, a hand squeezed my ankle. A voice begged, "Give me water. Get me water." A woman covered with soot and dirt was desperately clinging to my leg. I rushed into my home, where there was a well, and brought her water in a bowl. More and more voices rose up to ask for water.

So I kept giving it to them. Some of them thanked me and then died in front of me after drinking.

I was shocked and scared, and I immediately regretted what I had done. *Did I kill them? What is wrong with my water?* I thought.

That night my father said, "Children, don't give water to the injured, especially to the burned ones who are dehydrated, you know?"

"Of course I know that," my brothers and sister answered.

I held my breath with fear; I didn't want anyone to know I had already done just that. I kept my silence for thirty years, hiding this secret from my family. But even thirty years later, I had nightmares.

In spite of the many wounded and dying victims who lay on the stone steps, I climbed the hill to see the city, which was in ruins and on fire. I saw the smoke coming up all day long from the nearby park where my father, as a community leader, was cremating the victims.

Some wounded people I saw in the morning were chasing flies away. In the afternoon, maggots appeared on their wounds, and in the evening, some of them were taken to the park. In this park, my father and other civilian guards incinerated around three hundred bodies.

If I had gone to my school and had been looking up into the sky on the playground, I would have died or been terribly scarred like my classmates. If my brother's teacher hadn't changed the workplace from the area where Peace Park is now to the field near the station, he would be dead, too. If my brother hadn't come home that day, my parents would have entered ground zero soon after, and they would have died from the radiation aftereffects.

Even though I have no visible scars on my body now, I have suffered from this secret of giving the water to the victims every day since. I do not have physical scars; I have invisible scars.

*   *   *

3

REMEMBER PEARL HARBOR

1985

Peace has a price, and Jacob Beser knew the cost. Did the atomic bombs end the war? Who's to say? The radar countermeasures officer knew what he saw. He knew what the bombs did. He had to prepare himself every year when the anniversary grew closer. Reporters usually came calling for him and asking him questions—questions like, "What was it like being the only man in the world on both planes that dropped the atomic bomb?" "Do you feel guilty?" "Do you want to apologize?"

His answer was always the same: "That's not what we do."

The landing gear dropped, and the cameras started rolling. This year was different. This year, he decided he wanted to go back to Japan. ABC's *Good Morning America* brought him to Hiroshima to meet a survivor. His hardened eyes were stuck to the window, staring out at the

Japanese cities and villages arranged against the boundless hillsides. All those years ago, he had sat in the backs of the B-29s that carried their nuclear payloads. He saw the flash only through the covered window, and the towering mushroom cloud when he reached the main deck. For the first time in forty years, Lt. Beser had returned to Japan.

Beser was no longer a spritely, slight five-foot-five aspiring engineer. He was thicker. His once jet-black hair was still slicked back but had lightened to silver, and his eyes had hardened from locking up four decades of top secrets. He usually kept his cool, but during the majority of this trip, he hid behind dark-red aviator sunglasses perhaps incase he became emotional. His short-sleeved, button-down shirt was classy enough for an appearance on TV but casual enough to allow him to keep cool in the famous Japanese summer heat. He thought about what it would have been like to invade Japan in August instead of dropping the bomb and was relieved he didn't have to.

When Jacob Beser was allowed to, he did what few veterans could do. Since the minute the US government declassified the Manhattan Project, Lt. Beser had started to talk about the war.

It had been over twenty years since the United States and the Soviets came within a hairpin of nuclear war. The men in charge, in their smoke-filled war rooms that could have come from an episode of *Mad Men*, weren't selling advertisements; they were selling war—cold war. There were more than sixty thousand nuclear bombs, and they called it deterrence. Some called it a Mexican standoff. The world's power and security rested on the countries' decision not to destroy one other. There was no question in Beser's mind. *If humanity ever plays this game again, it will be a lot longer than forty years before anyone will be able to go on TV and discuss the effects.*

The ABC photographer filmed Beser's first steps in Hiroshima. He carried his own bags, which contained his Sony Walkman that he would use to record, a steno pad he would take notes on each night, and a week's worth of clothes. It was not unusual for Jake to record every step of a journey; his steno pad contained, along with the day's events, a complete list of his entire menu and drink orders for the whole trip—a rather lengthy list. When he was twenty-three, he kept records of *everything*. A pack rat, he held on to everything, even a personal phone record. His offices at home and at work were maintained by the "file by pile" system. But he knew exactly where everything was. He found order in the chaos.

Passersby eager to see someone important watched to see who was being filmed. Michiko, the production team coordinator assigned from ABC's Tokyo office, swiftly handled them.

"He is a World War II historian here to observe and commentate on the fortieth anniversary ceremony," she said, concealing his identity. "If Japanese people know who you are," she told him in the car, "you might get a reaction out of them. It's better if you remain neutral and not talk about it to people."

The film crew dropped their luggage at the ANA hotel, only a block away from Hiroshima's Peace Memorial Park. With not much time in between, Jake was taken to the Red Cross hospital, where most of the atomic-bomb victims still received treatment for their conditions.

Vice Director Dr. Kuramoto greeted them. He introduced the team to a number of patients who had been there for quite some time and some others who only came for short visits.

Dr. Kuramoto explained, "In this wing of the hospital, hibakusha—" as he referred to the survivors—"are all card carriers. In 1957, the Japanese government decided that anyone who would come forward and say that they had been in Hiroshima at the time of the bombing would qualify for a card and free medical care."

"What does hibakusha mean?" Jake asked.

"It literally translates to 'atomic bomb–affected person,'" replied the doctor, "but it also means 'person affected by radiation.'" He peered at Jake.

"Do you see a higher number of people here with diseases because of the radiation?" he asked.

"Actually, most of the cases our doctors deal with are the usual aging problems. With the exception of a slightly higher rate of some cancers, primarily breast for women and a few assorted others for men, there are no startling statistics to indicate that this survivor population is any worse off than any other large metropolitan population."

*   *   *

The next morning at six forty-five, the air was still cool and quiet at the Seiko clock tower, which would chime at eight fifteen. Jake and the crew met early to go directly to the Peace Park, where his interview with ABC News Correspondent Steve Fox would be filmed. The day of the anniversary was approaching, and more people flocked to the Peace Park. White tents were erected on the lawn, which usually lay green and empty. The Peace Park features the cenotaph memorial and a sprawling, lightly forested park dotted with various monuments to the dead. In the background rests the Atomic Bomb Dome, the skeletal remains of the domed cultural center. Jake and Steve sat on a shaded bench farther away from the commotion, and Michiko took off in a limo to pick up Shibama Tazu, the survivor whom Jake was going to meet.

"Yesterday you saw people in the hospital, suffering from something you caused. Does that give you any feelings of guilt?" asked Steve.

"No guilt, not at all," Jake said quickly. "These were acts of war. My father fought in the first war, and it was his generation that miserably failed and got us into the second war. My generation fought in the second war, and so far we haven't been able to hold back any of these brushfire wars. What really concerns me is that if things get out of hand—"

"I don't mean to interrupt," said Steve, "but back to the questions. When you saw the victims—"

"It didn't bother me. It was a war *they* started. We didn't ask for this, or Pearl Harbor, the death march in Bataan. These are things that, as Americans, made us quite upset."

"So speaking frankly, revenge and retaliation were your motivations at the time?" asked Steve.

"Well, you chose those words. I didn't," retorted Jake.

"Is it true?"

"Let's go back to the times. What was the national by-line? 'Remember Pearl Harbor.' Everything the country did was 'Remember Pearl Harbor.'"

*   *   *

4

THE CHAOS THAT FOLLOWED

1941

Jake didn't need to open his eyes to know the night before had been hard on him. The queasy twenty-year-old couldn't be sure if the pounding he was hearing came from the bedroom door or his throbbing head. "What did I—"

Thud…thud…knock. Knock. Knock.

It is *the door,* he thought. He pulled himself under the covers and dug his head deep under his pillows, shielding himself from the December chill and a headache that he knew would only get worse if he opened his eyes. *Could Pop already know?*

The night's events were swirling in his head. The gravity of his behavior had only just settled in. He might be facing expulsion from Johns Hopkins for tossing the dean's son into a freezing lake. He remembered leaving the scene of the crime quickly to find his classmates at the Chanticleer Club in Mount Vernon. The gang went for a howl, and the night became a blur of nightclubs, boilermakers, and five-cent oysters. He vaguely remembered driving his Model A back to his parents' house in Windsor Hill sometime after sunrise.

Nearly eight hours later, Jake was sleeping through the biggest news of the century. The ignored knocker stepped up his game to shouting. "Yakov, vake up! Yakov! Vake up!" One of Jake's foster brothers—though it was not documented who, we believe it was Egan, the one he was closest with—wrestled the locked door. Relieved it wasn't his father, and in no mood to fool around with his little brother, Jake rolled back over and tried to fall back asleep.

Since Hitler had risen to power, the Beser household had become a station of sorts. By 1941, Jake's mother, Rose, had taken in almost twenty children escaping the Nazi regime. A social worker and a foster child herself, Mrs. Beser was working with the German Jewish Children's Aid Society, acting to save children from concentration camps and find them permanent homes in Baltimore. Along with the slew of foster brothers and sisters from Europe, Jake had a younger set of twin sisters, Naomi and Sonya, and a little brother, Micky.

There wasn't much public information about what the Nazis were doing to their political enemies. In Germany, stories of death camps were only considered rumors until people started going missing and those not fit for the Nazi Party were relocated. Some of the foster kids were in denial, waiting for their parents to come back and get them.

Others knew what they were escaping and that there was no going back, at least not for the Jews.

When Otto Von Bismarck opened the ghettos and lifted the last restrictions on Prussian Jews in the late nineteenth century, the family story is that Jake Beser's great-grandfather Eliezer Besser left his family in Prussia behind to become US citizen Louis Beser, settling in Cincinnati, Ohio. He arrived in America with his brother right before the troubled nation was about to split into the Civil War. While the Besers laid their American roots, the Bessers continued to flourish in Germany until Jews were no longer safe.

Mrs. Beser was able to get papers for immigration for both her husband's extended family in Germany and her own in Eastern Europe. But despite how nearly impossible visas were to attain at the time, both families refused the opportunity. They didn't want to leave everything they knew as their life and home.

Though the letter has been lost, our family story, a common one, goes that they refused to come to America by saying something like, "This Nazi *phenomenon* is a passing phase. *Our* family never left during the Great War. Why would we leave now? Germany is our home. We are Germans."

Their refusal was the last contact the German Bessers had with the American Besers. The restless twenty-year-old Jake was anxious to fight Nazis. His people were being singled out and slaughtered. How could he sit back in a classroom when the world was going to war? It had happened throughout the history of the Jews. Now it was his turn to defend his people. He just had to convince his parents.

He tried everything he could to join up. He tried joining the British Royal Air Force, the French Air Force, and even the Royal Canadian Air Force. However, he was under twenty-one and needed his parents' permission. Each time he was met with, "Go back to school, contain yourself, and get your degree."

Now in his third year, he had grown restless. His run-in with the dean's son would be enough to get him expelled. If he got kicked out of Johns Hopkins, his parents might drop him off at the front lines themselves.

Nicholas, the father of the Beser household, bellowed in a low, booming voice from the living room, "Jacob, if you don't get up, you'll miss the war!"

Jake shot up in his bed, mystified. "War?" he shouted back.

"With Japan!" hollered Nicholas.

"*Japan?*" Jake reached for the door from his bed, and in burst his biological brother and his foster brother.

"The Japs hit Pearl Harbor!" shouted the boys, unaware of the gravity of what they were saying. "America is at war!"

"The Japs hit Pearl Harbor?" Jake was horrified at the unexpected news. "How bad is it?"

Nicholas walked right in and pulled open the window blinds. "It's hard to know *what's* going on," he said, ignoring his son's clear discomfort as the soft sunlight flooded into his room. "It's all still unfolding, but it sounds bad."

Jake took a cold shower and put on a pot of black coffee. The fog began to lift, and he was able to comprehend what H. V. Kaltenborn and Gabriel Heatter were saying on the radio: "So far as is known, the attacks on Hawaii and Manila were made wholly without warning when both nations were at peace."

As the news unfolded, Jake made up his mind, but he waited until breakfast the next morning to announce his decision. While members of his family filtered through the kitchen and went off to their normal Monday duties, Jake sat there until he blurted out, "Mom, I know what you're going to say, but—"

"Don't even think about it, Jacob," said his mother, anticipating the statement. She had dedicated her work to getting children out of the path of war, and she was staunchly against sending her own toward it.

"But, Ma!" he pleaded.

"I've said it once, and I'll say it again. Combat flying is no place for a good Jewish boy. What kind of job is that? You will get yourself killed," she wailed.

"But you dropped out of Columbia University to go to France in the World War. You *knew* you had to!"

"*I* joined a field social-service unit of the Jewish Welfare Board to serve with the AEF," contested his mother. "I didn't sign up for a death sentence!"

Jake turned to his dad for support. "Pop, Procter and Gamble's loss was the AEF's gain when you became a cannon cocker in the Big Red One. You were in the army's first division!"

Nicholas never ran out of war stories. "We were the first American unit to join the French in the Marne Valley and engage the enemy," he said, "and on the other side of the front lines in the opposite trenches were my cousins!"

"Dad, that happened to a ton of people. It's Baltimore; there are more Germans in Hanover, Maryland, than there are in Hanover, Germany."

"The point is, Jake, I know what you want to do. I don't like it any more than your mother, but I can't argue with you, either. If you want to enlist, I'll take you to do it."

"But no combat training," Mrs. Beser chimed in. "Nicholas, make sure he enlists in a communications school or something mechanical. Put your engineering degree to good use."

By noon, December 8, the Hopkins dropout was sworn in as Private Jacob Beser, with the accompaniment of his father, and told to await a call announcing the formation of his class of cadets. He withdrew from school without prejudice. His run-in with the dean's son went undocumented, forgotten after Pearl Harbor and the chaos that followed.

* * *

5

Teruko Yahata, Eight Years Old

Aboard the Peace Boat, eight other survivors, a youth communicator, the trip coordinator, and I as a web reporter formed the project taking hibakusha to give their testimony. When we reached Central America, having originated from Japan, Mrs. Teruko Yahata was feeling the overview effect often experienced by astronauts when they look at earth from space. "We have sailed across so many beautiful seas, under beautiful skies, and docking in beautiful lands," she exclaimed in awe to the audience of the El Salvadorian Foreign Ministry. "We all share this precious earth, yet we are bent on destroying it. How many people need to become atomic-bomb survivors before we ban these weapons?" I pray that no one should survive atomic weapons. You cannot imagine the horror it is to live with this experience for seventy years.

One night on our way back to Japan, somewhere in the middle of our twenty days at sea, I was relaxing with Mrs. Yahata, practicing my Japanese on the eighth-floor Casablanca bar. The topic of my grandfather came up. Yahata tearfully had her own secret to admit. She needed a translator, and we had none with us, so I waited until the next day during our scheduled interview for her to reveal to me her guilt about Pearl Harbor.

Before the Pacific War started, I was living with my mom and my father, my sister, my two little brothers, my grandmother, and my great-grandmother. My mom, a dutiful wife, was traditionally Japanese in that sense. She supported my dad in everything he needed, and my father respected her and loved us. He took us for long walks and to amusement parks on his days off.

One day, my father's cousin came home to my aunt's house. He was a soldier, and he requested, "Please take care of my Yanagi Gori basket, and if something happens to me, you will receive my belongings." He said nothing else and left.

In Japan, December 8, 1941, is a day that will live in infamy, Nineteen hours ahead of Hawaii time, the Japanese navy, my cousin in tow, set out to successfully attack Pearl Harbor. War was declared, and in Japan, there was a huge celebration. People felt proud that the Japanese had provoked the Western power.

A few days later, my cousin returned home and boasted to my family about what he did. "Did you hear the news? I did it. I was there! I bombed Pearl Harbor!" He was happy about what he did, and we were proud of him. I was only eight years old, and all I knew was that he had helped my country do something good. He bragged about the details of the top-secret mission, saying, "There was a ship in Hiroshima's port that took me to Chitose in Hokkaido at night. From there, we took off to Pearl Harbor and into history!" Six months later, he died in the ocean in a fight with Americans near Taiwan.

As the war intensified, my father had to leave home to work in China. He worked for the Meiji candy factory, but during the war, they shifted their responsibility from confectionaries. He oversaw the shipment and storage of the military's foodstuff grown throughout the expanding Japanese empire. All of Japan served the emperor and thus owed supplies for the strength of the military and the success of the war.

On August 2, Father returned to Hiroshima. He had been in Tokyo on a business trip and planned his route to China via Hiroshima Port. He was supposed to go back the next day, but every port, including Tenzin and Taiwan, closed down. No ships in; no ships out.

On August 5, Father took us to the beach for some quality family time. The whole country was fervently strengthening the empire for the war effort. My brothers probably should have been home practicing katana bamboo-stick fighting for the impending invasion. We were practically alone, and we were happy, albeit briefly. I don't remember how blue the ocean was, or the waves we saw; I just remember feeling safe with my father.

At around seven the next morning, an air-raid alert went out. We listened to the radio to see if the warning was lifted. We didn't hear any updates. I went outside to ask my neighbor if it had lifted. As I turned my back to return to the house, I saw a light in the sky, like a fluorescent blue lamp turning on for all of Hiroshima. I knew it was something dangerous, so I instinctively covered my eyes, ears, and nose before I lost consciousness.

I woke up, though I don't know how much later. I saw the walls broken down and the house a mess and smoke billowing from inside. I teetered on the edge of consciousness, and my mother called out, "Come here. Come here. Follow my voice!"

I looked around and saw shards of glass the size of tables stuck into the walls like arrows. I had been thrown five meters back toward my house. I ran toward my mother's voice, and she covered all of us with the futon mat. All of our family members were underneath and alive. My parents were giant birds, protecting us with their wings. I still have the feeling of the importance of family because of this. "If we die, we die together!" my mother yelled.

We had never experienced such a big bomb, and we thought a second or third would come. Next to the river, our house stood by a larger house that used to always cast a shadow on our property, and my mother would complain that sunlight wouldn't reach our garden because of it. But this shadow had spared our house from the flash and thus from burning down from the incredible heat.

I must have hit my head. I don't remember when. It was bleeding, so my mom wiped my face, and my dad treated me. My father also treated my grandmother and mom, but they had suffered only surface wounds. We were determined to make our way to an air-raid shelter. We left our house, and saw that the whole area was destroyed. The air-raid shelter was either too full or too dangerous, so we went toward the mountain.

All of the soldiers who were working there were half naked and burned. They begged, "Give me water."

Some who walked by refused and said, "You'll die if you drink it," but the desperate soldiers begged anyway.

It started to rain, drop by drop, turning into a downpour. The dying opened their mouths to catch the water; children stood in it for relief. The raindrops were not clear but black. We didn't know it then, but this black rain was infused with uranium. My family went back toward our house to avoid getting wet. Toward the bridge, I saw one girl crying and screaming by herself. Her hair stood on its ends, covered in ash. Then, a lot of people ran toward us from behind her. I couldn't look at them. Their faces, hands, and legs were all burned, ripped apart, with skin hanging from their fingertips and dragging at their ankles.

The river was congested with people wading in the waters for relief, as well as with the dead and dying. Worst of all, people desperately drank from the river. I happened upon my dad's cousin, a young boy in middle school. He had a black face but white teeth. He smiled, relieved to find us, and said, "I came to pick you up and take you to our house!" We wove through a kilometer of debris until we reached the tree line, which must have been shielded from the bomb's blast.

I will always remember my aunt's house, the bubbling streams, the cicada, and the quiet wood. Before, we had been in hell, but experiencing nature on the mountain untouched by the bomb was like being in heaven. My dad said that because I had this wound on my forehead, he took me to Koi Elementary, where they were treating injuries.

Koi Elementary was my former elementary school, which we hadn't attended toward the end of the war. All of the rooms and halls and any other spaces inside were used for the injured. I went to my old classrooms, but the rooms were full of swollen faces and burned bodies. I still remember that some people's faces were swollen and burned to the point that they couldn't open their eyes, and someone was walking around with slices of peaches to feed them.

Dead people were carried into the yards, thrown into dugout ditches, and burned to ash. My memory of Koi had always been of springtime, when the sports field was covered in cherry blossoms and the children were happy and playing, but this time the same field was filled with bodies being cremated. I just watched the people burning. The smoke and fire were too shocking. I didn't feel any emotion, and I wasn't affected by the putrid smell. I just stood there, watching. My father took us home, and higher up in the mountains, we could see the whole city still burning, burning into the night.

*   *   *

6

IT'LL COME OUT IN THE WASH

1943

*T*hings have a way of happening fast in the army, and then it becomes "hurry up and wait," thought Beser as he waited for his transport to take him to his next assignment. *You can never know what to expect.*

Private Beser and his partner, Bill Eades, spent all day arranging their transportation and clearing their posts. Bright and early Tuesday morning, they were dropped off at an intersection in the middle of nowhere with all of their worldly possessions. They waited at the entrance road to the Boca Raton Club and US-1, the Dixie Highway, for the Trailways bus that would take them to Orlando. They were simply told by a commanding officer to "be sure you flag it down," with no alternative given if they didn't.

Beser had placed fifth in his class at the Army Air Corps in Scott Airfield Base. While most would be pleased with this accomplishment, he was frustrated. This meant that he would not be placed in the way of combat. He was assigned to MIT and Harvard for research. His commanding officer heard his concerns and gave him an alternative. No combat, but if he went to a training facility in Boca Raton, Florida, and completed the required certifications, he could get his choice of placements from there. He joined to kill Nazis, not to sit out the war in a classroom.

In the later thirties and early forties, the Allies were engaged in a Battle of the Beams with the Nazis, who were flying sophisticated night flights over the United Kingdom. Beser and the other Americans, however, were training and perfecting radio detection and ranging, or radar, for themselves. They used a device that sends a burst of radio energy and measures the time it takes for that energy to impinge on a target, or enemy aircraft, and be reflected back. One could track, control, or attack any target with the control of the right radio frequency.

A security blanket had been drawn over their work, so after study hours, all of their books and notebooks were taken away and locked in a safe for the night. The course was labeled Radio-S Training, and the words "advanced electronics" and "radar" were never said outside of the classroom. Beser spent three months in Boca Raton before he mastered the new art and became one of the best and brightest officers in the field.

Once the cadets mastered a piece of equipment, they took it out on antisubmarine patrol to learn how to use it. Eventually, they advanced as far as simulated night fighting, flying simulated night intercepts with startling accuracy. Slowly, they developed and improved the emerging technology. The wiry young 9.8/10 private had become a wiry young 9.8/10 lieutenant who felt sure he would get his choice of assignment.

After three months, Beser picked up his orders to leave with Lt. William B. Eades Jr. for an undefined assignment at the Army Air Forces School of Applied Tactics in Orlando, Florida. The orders were full of deliberate omissions disguising the fact that they were two airborne radar officers. Their mission remained unclear, but Beser welcomed *any* advancement in his military career.

The bus was due at the stop around eight in the morning, and it was right on time, kicking up a trail of dust as it made its way from base to base, delivering various cadets to their new assignments. Beser and Eades loaded their belongings, which included two footlockers, two flight bags, two musette bags, and paper sacks carrying assorted junk that they had not found room for elsewhere. Their briefcases, handcuffed to their wrists, contained all of their top-secret school notes, papers, and books. They could not remove the handcuffed luggage until they arrived at their destination twelve hours later and located a secure safe. Within an hour of arrival, they were in their basic overnight quarters (BOQ), where they could finally uncuff their belongings from their wrists. Their orders were so blacked out that nobody knew what to do with them.

For the next fifteen months, Beser was stuck in and around Florida. A fast learner, he discovered that if he kept his ears up and his head down, he could pick up assignments. He managed his way into the bombardment department and was assigned duties as a test and development project officer. The lieutenant also started training cadres of corps personnel to form new organizations to send over to Europe and the Pacific as fast as they could get the experienced ones back, rotating them. While some of his fellow instructors had been to combat and back again, Beser had only read about it. Half the students in each class had been there once, too. He got transferred back to Boca Raton temporarily to become a certified radar countermeasures officer, the latest and greatest certification that airborne radar officers could attain. Along with the rating came flying status, which not only brought a 50 percent increase in pay and a closer association with the flying end of the business but also got Beser one step closer to combat. His Nazi vendetta was taking longer than anticipated to redress, but his feelings were only getting stronger. The Besers had officially lost contact with all of his father's German family, and they assumed the worst.

Nobody paid attention to Beser's whereabouts. Project officers such as himself would get samples of faulty equipment, verify the issue, fix it, and then report back to the manufacturer about it. He could pick up any job he wanted and leave freely, and no one would notice. So he did just that.

When the lieutenant got his chance, he caught a ride up to the Pentagon, hoping he could convince someone to transfer him to a combat unit. The chief communications officer of the air force told him, "Go back where you belong."

Nicholas Beser's friend was an aide to Gen. Ulio, the adjutant general, and was able to get his son a meeting. Gen. James Alexander Ulio, with four stars on his shoulder, had spent the majority of his life in army administration. He was the man who signed every general order through the Pentagon. Whether it was one executed there or filtered down through lesser commands, he could do anything he wanted with people. Beser was certain his audience with the general would get him to combat.

Gen. Ulio took one look at this brash twenty-two-year-old in front of him and knew exactly what he wanted, but he asked, "Where is it you want to go?"

"Sir, I want to see combat. I want to be deployed to Europe, sir."

"Sounds good to me," he replied without a fight. "Wait outside while I retrieve your file." Ulio sent his sergeant major to the basement of the Pentagon, where the records of everyone in uniform were stored.

Half an hour later, the sergeant major came back to see the general. Beser saw Ulio talking to the aide outside his office, the two of them confusedly shaking their heads. Finally, he was motioned into the room. The general looked at him with a slight smirk and said, "I'm sorry, son.

I don't understand it, but your records have been flagged. *I* can't touch you."

The general may or may not have known why Beser was flagged, but if he did, he wasn't letting him know. This made Beser a little more upset than usual, but Gen. Ulio's hands were tied. He was trying to contain his wry smile at the frustrated lieutenant when he said, "Return to your station, son. I'm sure it'll come out in the wash."

* * *

7

JONG KEUN LEE, SEVENTEEN YEARS OLD

In 1910, the Korean Peninsula was annexed by Japan in a trade deal that ended with Japan having free range of Korean land, crops, and its people. Many Koreans began changing their names to Japanese names. By 1939, it was policy, part of Japan's attempt at cultural assimilation. Lee-san isn't known by Lee-san to most of his friends in Hiroshima. It's the name he uses when he tells his survival story. For most of his adult life, Lee-san hid two things from his friends: that he was a hibakusha and that he was a Korean national. Lee-san's story didn't start and end with the atomic bomb. Because he was Korean, he was discriminated against. Seventy years later, at eighty-seven years old, Lee-san travels the world to speak out against the dangers of nuclear weapons and discrimination. He always wears a splash of color, be it bright orange shoes or a purple scarf, because he wants to express on the outside how young he feels on the inside. Wherever he goes, he runs. When he joined Peace

Boat to give testimonies, he ran around the top deck of the ocean liner as it cruised around the world. When he came to New York with Hibakusha Stories, the NGO run by Disarmament Educatior Dr. Kathleen Sullivan, he ran around the graveyard before dawn. He received a quick chastising from his host the project's founder, who was intent on making Lee-san aware of the things you do and do not do alone in Brooklyn before the sun comes up. Lee-san wouldn't have any of it. He knows how to take care of himself. He has been doing so his whole life.

In the early days before the invasion, my father and my mother had a farm in Korea. When the Japanese foray into Asia strengthened, the invaders forced everybody to abandon their normal crops like rice and instead burn wood to make charcoal to support the Japanese troops. My father and his neighbors wanted to plant other crops, but they were forced not to. He decided to take my family to Japan. He hoped life would be better there.

I was born in the small village of Yoshiwa, two hours outside of the center of Hiroshima. I hated that place. It wasn't a kind place for me. Everyone knew me, and they knew I was Korean. Koreans used to all be called Chōsen. They wouldn't use my name, and that wasn't even the worst of it.

"Hey, Chōsen!" a townsperson once said. "Come and stand in front of me!"

"What do you want?" I asked.

"Don't speak. Just stand right here." He pointed to the ground. When I complied, the old man whipped out his penis and pissed all over me.

When I reached the sixth grade, the war had already started. We moved to Saka, and I transferred schools. Mitsubishi shipbuilding was going to build a dock there. They needed the labor, so my father became a headhunter and recruited workers for them. Father was an intellectual who knew how to start a business. He was quite successful, too. He was well connected in the Korean community, most of whom were forcibly removed to Japan, and they needed the work, anyway.

I decided to go by my Japanese name when we moved to the city. I had heard that a lot of people hid their Korean names. I hid mine, too, but my teachers knew the truth. Getting work was difficult for me because of that. I had to take an exam to work at the Testudo Railway. I passed the exam, and my teacher gave me the results to take to the factory. They were enclosed in an envelope. I shouldn't have opened it. It should have been sealed, but I wanted to know if I had passed. I opened it anyway and found out that not only had I passed the exam, but that my nationality was written on the paper. My teacher had written that I was Chōsen, and I crossed it out. I got the job, but I have been hiding my nationality since.

My education ended with primary school. Afterward, I started to work at the railway company, Hiroshima Testudo, mending train lines. I was fifteen years old. I moved out of my parents' house and into the company dormitory under my Japanese name. Around the time I got the job in Hiroshima City, my father made up his mind to close his recruitment office in Saka and move to Hatsukaichi City, between Hiroshima and Miyajima Island.

One of the benefits of being under employ of the railroad was that I rode the trains for free. I often commuted from Hatsukaichi to Hiroshima. Life became better for me. I made friends, even though they thought I was Japanese. Nobody knew I was Korean, and no one could tell the difference between Korean and Japanese. On the morning of August 6, I actually missed my train. Some people missed their trains and it saved their lives, but it almost cost me mine. My mother and I were arguing, and I was late.

I entered the city on the train from Koi Station to Hiroshima Station. From Hatsukaichi, I used to ride the streetcar, but on the morning of the sixth, I missed it. I had to change trains at Koi Station on the western end of the city. From Koi, I took the local streetcar to Matoba and walked the rest of the way. I worked near what is now the Hiroshima Toyo Carp's baseball stadium but what was then a big railway compound.

I had just crossed a few steps onto the other side of the Bridge when a flash—a yellow, bright flash—surrounded me. I was blinded for what seemed like a few seconds. When lightning strikes, it lasts for an instant. But this lasted longer. For five seconds, all I could see was light.

I had been taught that in the event of a bomb, I had to put two fingers over my eyes, my thumbs in my ears, and my small fingers in my nose and lie facedown on the ground. I lay there still and didn't move. I don't know how long it was, but when I opened my eyes, it was night. I couldn't understand why it was so dark. I hadn't lain down for even an hour, but the sun had disappeared. The back of my head was so hot. I heard my hair sizzling. My rail man's hat was burned black. The back of my light-blue, button-down shirt was burned off, but I didn't feel pain. I didn't feel anything. I thought that a bomb had dropped right behind me.

That day, I wore my hat and glasses and carried my bento lunch box. I didn't care about the glasses, but the bento was crucial. Food was scarce back then, so I needed to find it. After regaining consciousness, I couldn't recognize my surroundings. Everything had collapsed. However, my first thought was, *I have to find my bento.*

The blast had come from behind me, so I figured that my bento had to be in front of me, somewhere. I found it, but it was at least fifty meters away. I was in a dangerous area, so I began to seek shelter. I went down to the river under the bridge, and already two or three people were there. So far, I hadn't seen many people, maybe four or five total. One of them immediately said, "This was a new type of bomb. It had to be." He then yelled, "Something's happened to your face. Your skin's changed color!"

With his words, all of the feeling returned to my face, my hair, my legs, my fingers, and my back. All of it seared and stung at once, as if his words had brought my nerves back to life. We left and tried to go to my factory. In those days, there was another railroad that isn't running anymore. It was a special track to dispatch soldiers. On the way, all of the houses were either fractured or completely collapsed. I could hear many people stuck under the houses, crying for help, but I couldn't help them. I felt sorry, but I had to keep going. I had to make it to safety.

I saw a man slumped over the railway tracks. He was still wearing clothes, and he wasn't burned. I shook him to see if he would wake up, but he wouldn't move. I turned him over. He was already dead. I wondered why I was burned but alive and he was uninjured but dead. I saw the factory still standing, so I left him.

I met my colleagues inside. They were unharmed. They hadn't missed *their* trains and had gotten to work on time. Surprised to see me, they asked what had happened outside. We used to put locomotive oil on burns to treat them, so while I explained what I saw, they covered my face with it. The oil, however, didn't help.

While my workplace was in east Hiroshima, my home was in the west, so I needed to walk through the city to get home. There were a couple of us who had to get to that part of town, so at around four that afternoon, we set out.

We walked toward Hiroshima University. We skirted around the entire affected zone and crossed Meiji Bridge, Sumioshi Bridge, and Kandon Bridge. Parts of them were actively burning, and other parts of them were already burned down, but we were able to cross. There were so many dead and dying, even animals like people's horses, but I didn't look down in the waters. I knew there were more there. I heard only later that the rivers were so full of people, you couldn't even see the water.

The bridges were bottlenecked. Hordes of people were fleeing the city. They were dreadful: their skin was peeling off, their hair was burned, and many of them were naked. It is still very difficult for me to explain it. How can I explain what four-thousand-degree-Celsius light does to people standing outside? How can I explain what five-hundred-mile-per-hour winds can do?

Glass was projected into bullets. Some people were pierced with pieces of debris, almost perfectly in line with the angles at which they had been standing in relation to the blast. People gathered by the bridge to be seen by anyone who knew them. No one was crossing; they were just standing there. For some their internal muscles showing. All they were saying was, "Water. Water."

I can still see those people on the bridges. The sight was unforgettable. Their eyes—I'll never forget their eyes. Their eager eyes just staring at me, hoping I was their family, hoping I would claim them and give them some relief.

I just kept walking. Nothing to drink; just kept walking. I had to get home. I didn't drink water until I got home, and I didn't get home until 11:00 p.m. My parents were not there. I asked my younger brother, "Where are Mom and Dad?"

"Oh, they went to the city center to find you," he said.

The trains weren't working, obviously, so I had to walk back, but my parents had entered the city on foot and then slowly made their way back to our family's house. They got as far as Koi before they turned back. Father tried to get to the side near the hypocenter, but everything was burning—a sea of fire—so it was impossible.

Before dark, Father made his way back. Even in such an area, he could see the fires of Hiroshima. Father and Mother had split up. When I returned my brother told me he was hungry, but we had no food. Mom didn't return home until the morning. I didn't sleep. I couldn't. She was surprised to see that I was alive, and she was so happy to see me, even though I was burned. The first meal after Mother returned was rice and boiled radishes.

There was a Tetsudo hospital near Hatsukaichi Station, and I could go for free because I was a Tetsudo worker. They had run out of medicine. All they had was *akachin*, a red liquid lotion. The akachin turned hard and peeled off when new flesh appeared, but it took a long time to heal around my eyes. My skin was boiled.

I could chase the flies away from my face and hands, but I couldn't see them. They laid eggs that turned into maggots—so many maggots on my neck and back. It was so painful and miserable. I could feel them moving in my skin. My mother had to pick them out with chopsticks. She and I both cried through the experience. She whimpered, "I can't stand seeing you like this. It would have been better if you had died."

Then one day, I noticed my hair had fallen out, and I got diarrhea. I heard these were symptoms of the atomic-bomb disease and that I would die any day.

Each day that I pulled on my hair and it didn't fall out, I would think, *I will live another day.*

*   *   *

8

Never Going to Be Rejoined Again

1944

Beser had no choice but to return to his post in Florida. He couldn't ask his commanding officers why his file was flagged because no one knew he had gone to the Pentagon. The dismayed lieutenant went back to the bombardment division of the School of Applied Tactics and to his model bomb group unnoticed.

As the cadres came through, they had to go on more simulated missions Beser led, as he demonstrated what they talked about in the classroom. Beser thought it was ironic that he had yet to face the combat he was teaching others countermeasures for.

The Ninth Bomb Group had a training center for the air force in Fairmont, Nebraska, to transition to B-29s and eventually go overseas to fight Japan. Beser told the commanding officer of the group, whom he knew very well, "Jim, you know, I would love to go with you."

"Why not, Beser? Come with us!" he said.

Beser wanted to get lost in the shuffle. Everything they did down in Orlando was internal and wouldn't filter back, so he figured he could get to Fairmont. Without telling the commanding officer about being denied transfer in DC, the desperate young lieutenant accepted the offer.

By February, Fairmont, Nebraska, population twenty-three, including the graveyard, had welcomed the addition of a top-secret airbase carved out of the biggest cornfield Beser had ever seen. It was a perfect testing ground for the experimental B-29.

The problem was, the powers that be hadn't delivered any test planes. Instead, the men of the 504th were practicing with war-weary B-17s, the baby brothers of the B-29s. The B-17 had an excellent record in Europe, but it was not the B-29 superfortress.

When the first B-29s arrived, they were X-Bs, or experimental versions of the aircraft that another wing had trained on. They couldn't have been any worse if they were war weary. They were underpowered, with every problem a new airplane could have, but the worst part was that every time they took off from the ground, they caught fire. In the middle of the night, when engine fires kept hitting the ground, Beser would wake up in a night terror, or the screaming meemies, as he called them. It took about three months of testing until they got a halfway decent aircraft running.

By this time, Beser knew that there was nothing he could do about his position. Having exhausted his options, he took

NEVER GOING TO BE REJOINED AGAIN 1944

a leave and went to Chicago for some R and R. He was supposed to be gone three days. Seven days later, he had not
even bothered to call his superiors to say he wasn't coming
back yet. The army has a name for this, AWOL, or absent
without leave. It's a punishable offense that can bring on a
court-martial. *No sense giving them time to be mad at me.* He
didn't call; he simply returned as fast as he could get back.

Beser's commanding officer liked him, so he intervened
before the higher-ups could have their way. Instead of being court-martialed, he was taken out of the 504th and put
into the 393rd squadron as a punitive action. The squadron
commander was a seasoned combat veteran, an excellent
flier, and a stern disciplinarian. "A couple of weeks with
Tom Classen oughta straighten you out," they said to him.

After three weeks, Beser started to actually enjoy his
time with his new commander, who he came to know
and respect. The commandant of Fairmont Army Airfield
published General Order No. 254. Paragraph seven of
that order had the bombshell. "All of the personnel of the
393rd Squadron are hereby ordered to report no later than
September fifteenth to Wendover Field, Utah, for temporary duty complete with all organizational equipment." The
inclusion that they would take all organizational equipment
with them and the statement that no per diem would be paid
while at Wendover were clues to the fact that the 393rd and
the 504th were never going to be rejoined again.

* * *

9

TOSHIKO TANAKA, SIX YEARS OLD

From a young age, Toshiko decided to forget what she witnessed in Hiroshima and to never look back. She didn't want to dwell on the horrors of her past. She watched others around her eat themselves away with despair. That wouldn't be her. She pushed those feelings down and picked up a talent for enamel art, but no matter what, she couldn't forget what had happened on that August day. A plane would fly over, and she would do a double take. When she barbecued tomatoes, the skin on the tomatoes would blacken and peel, and for a second, she would see a face she remembered. Her burns had faded over time, but her invisible scars were permanent. As an artist, she relished the creation of enamel pieces so abstract and unique that nobody knew she was hiding messages in them. The messages weren't for anyone else but herself. It wasn't until 2007 to 2009, when she traveled with Peace Boat to thirty countries, that she began to open up. Among the people she met along the way

*were victims of war. Their positive attitudes and ability
to convey their own horrific experiences inspired Toshiko
to remember her own and start talking about them.*

I was nearly seven when the bomb dropped. At the time, we Japanese had nothing to eat, and people were poor. Even if the A-bomb had not been dropped, we would have had to surrender. It was worse than it is right now in North Korea.

Even though there was war, I had a happy life as a kid. My favorite place to be was where the Peace Park is now. My house was there. It was called Nakajima. One American came to Hiroshima years later, and he said to me, "Luckily, the atomic bomb dropped over the Peace Park. There must not have been much damage."

"That's not true," I told him. "This used to be the busiest market in Hiroshima. It is forbidden to sell here now out of respect for the dead."

My grandmother and I would pick spring vegetables at a really small park in Nakajima. We picked vegetables for the *ryokan* (traditional inn) that was called Hara-Ryokan. It was not lucky that the bomb dropped here.

Ujina Port used to be a big port where the soldiers were dispatched to fight for Japan. Soldiers came together to our inn from all over Japan. They would come, and then they would ship off and die. I never saw anyone more than once.

Shortly before the bombs were dropped, we were ordered out of the property. The roads were being widened as planned escape routes in case of a firebombing, and Hara-Ryokan was in the way. We moved near my mother's family, 2.3 kilometers away in Ushita, only six days before the bomb was dropped. All of my friends from elementary school, who were in the middle of the hypocenter, died. If we had stayed longer, we too would have died.

From our new home, I saw the first B-29 flying away from Hiroshima City. I was relieved, so I went outside to head to my school. While I was on my way, I saw the plane *Enola Gay*. One of my friends screamed, "Hey! There's another bomber!" That's when I saw the flash. And I was instantly blinded. I couldn't see anything, but I felt myself being thrown away. Instinctively, I covered my eyes, and my hands and neck were burned, though the burns are not visible anymore without close inspection. My hair was burned and stood on its ends like I had been electrocuted.

I think I survived because of the water system. It had stopped after the bomb, but I found some water gushing out of a broken pipe. I poured water on my arms and saw blisters forming.

Shortly afterward, I went back home. With my hair burned, my face blackened because of the ash, and my clothes tattered and ripped, I just barely made it. My mother saw me but didn't even recognize me. She put cooking oil on my wounds because we thought it was good for them. Cooking oil was very expensive at the time and usually required one to have fine goods to trade, like a nice kimono, in order to afford it. However, my parents owned an inn, so we had a big bottle of it. We put on ointments, as well, because we had no real medicine or doctors. It was so painful, but we were desperate.

My aunt, who was twenty-two at the time, had lived in Ushita with us. But on the morning of August 6, she had to go to the center of the city in part of the forced mobilization of Hiroshima citizens to demolish buildings for widening the escape routes, and we never saw her again. Likewise, my uncle's family of six lived in the Hachobori area near the modern Fukuya department store. They all died.

The first night following the bomb, I had a very high fever and lost consciousness for four to six days. My mother thought I would die. We didn't have any doctors, and my father was off fighting in the war and couldn't attend to us. She fed me water and not much else. It was all she could do.

Even though I went unconscious that night, I remember clearly what I saw before fading. People were evacuating and coming toward my house in Ushita, away from the blast zone. They were nearly dead, speechless, and burned. They were like marching ghosts. The bridge called Kanda-bashi, which is still there now, was broken in half because the blast had come from underneath. The survivors of the initial blast walked over the broken bridge. Those who couldn't make it across fell into the river and died.

Many died in front of my house on the street, including children. It was so hot, the surface of the road was burning. Everyone who died had skin ripped and hanging to their nails, their arms outstretched.

My mother was in the bathroom when the bomb went off. God was looking out for her. The structure was very strong, and she had been sitting low. She later said that the wall was totally destroyed, too. She saw this blue fire or flash come through the wall. If she had been hit by the flash directly, she would have burned to death.

My mother had to go to the city office that day for registration concerning our family's recent move—documenting the change of address and so on. My mother's older sister, my aunt, was going to come to the house to take care of my sisters. I was in school, but they were still little and needed someone to take care of them. However, my aunt was late because she had gone back home to find a tray for collecting horse manure; Japan had nothing at the time, but horse feces were nutritious and made good fertilizer, so whenever some was lying in the street, people would rush to get it. Because of the delay, my mother hadn't set out for the city center. While waiting for her sister to arrive, she went to the bathroom before the day's journey, the bathroom that saved her life. My aunt's and my mother's lives were spared because of horse shit.

*   *   *

10

WHAT DOES HE KNOW THAT I DON'T?

1944

The troop train carrying the bulk of the men of the 393rd from Fairmont, Nebraska, had been sitting in a freight yard in Salt Lake City since about 0400 hours. It sat on the track adjacent to a trainload of Italian prisoners of war. While they waited, with both trains needing new engines, the soldiers traded their American cigarettes for the hot pastries being fed to the Italians. The 393rd was about twelve miles from their destination.

At 1000 hours, a new engine was hooked to their train, and they moved out of the yard, once again headed west. The scenery from Fairmont to eastern Colorado was flat and unimpressive. It got interesting from Denver to Laramie, Wyoming, and continued that way on into Salt Lake City. Now on this last leg of their trip, they were being set up for Wendover, Utah. They rolled into the isolated Bonneville Salt Flats. In almost every direction for a hundred miles, there was nothing except a seldom-used train line, a desert, and a mountainous horizon. It was the perfect area for a military base.

Wendover was wholly unromantic. Beser looked out the right side of the train and saw a highway, a gas station complete with a restaurant attached, several other stores, and not much else. Out the left side of the train, he saw the base, which was an airfield and a collection of barracks, Quonsets, hangars, and a chapel, all set against a small brown mountain (or a large brown hill). Beser quipped to another officer, "If North America ever needs an enema, they could insert the tube here."

After unloading the train and getting assigned to their quarters, the troops found the bar at the officers' club. Wendover lay across the border of Nevada and Utah. On the Nevada side, the Stateline Hotel had a bar and casino. On the Utah side, outdoor types could go hiking, hunting, and fishing in the glacial mountain lakes, if time allowed. For everyone else, there was a restaurant, Spike's. The base held an officers' club, a noncoms club, a large rec hall for enlisted men, a theater showing the latest first-run movies, and an occasional traveling USO show.

Beser and his crew set up right away. He staked out a space and an office in the engineering hangar where he and Lt. Elroy Homa set up their squadron electronics facility. Since the radar equipment was classified, their shop would require a guard around the clock. Inside, their men immediately began making test benches and equipment mock-ups. Within a week, their two sections were in full operation.

Some strange faces began showing up shortly after they did—white coats and military personnel. By the middle of their first week at Wendover, the strangers had multiplied exponentially. No one knew where the men were coming from or what they were doing, but the men in the 393rd were about to find out.

On Monday, September 25, 1944, the entire squadron was called to the base theater at 0900 hours. The new strangers joined the congregation. A short fellow about Beser's height who was wearing the silver leaf of a lieutenant colonel and command pilot's wings introduced himself as Lt. Col. Paul Tibbets and called the meeting to order.

"I'm your new commanding officer," he announced to the group. "You have all been selected to form the cadre of a new type of combat group, one that will be self-sufficient and can operate anywhere in the world. You will be asked to carry out a mission that, if successful, will bring the war to a rapid conclusion. You must trust me. You will not be told what your mission is until we are ready to perform it. You are going to be asked to do a lot of hard work over the next few months in order to bring our skills and performance to the highest possible level. You are to be reorganized, and some new people will be coming in.

"May I remind you that security is of the utmost importance? What you see here, what you hear here, when you leave here, let it stay here. There will be *no* second chances where security breaches are concerned. Gentlemen, much is going to be expected of you. If it all works out, it will have all been worth it. For the next two weeks, the entire 393rd squadron will be on furlough, including most of your officers. Those who are required to be here to help in the reorganization have already been notified. Oh, and one more thing before dismissing you: I want to inform Lt. Jacob Beser to please meet me in my office in fifteen minutes."

Maj. Classen came up to Beser at once. He gave one disapproving glance at his flight-line clothes and suggested gruffly, "On the way up to base headquarters, stop at your barracks and get into class-A uniform. It just might be useful." Confused, the young lieutenant wondered, *What does he know that I don't?*

* * *

11

KEIJIRO MATSUSHIMA, SIXTEEN YEARS OLD

I first met Keijiro in 2011. He spoke at the Hiroshima Museum's arranged English language testimony session the day after Mrs. Ogura and was also willing to speak privately with me, though we didn't need a translator. He had been an English teacher for over forty years and was fluent in my native tongue. He told me that he went to Tinian for one of the 509th reunions in 2005 and asked a serviceman for forgiveness, but he doesn't remember whom. The crewman refused.

"I don't want forgiveness anymore. I just wish that people could hear what happened underneath the mushroom cloud as many times as it takes until people demand we get rid of these weapons." Every year that I returned to Hiroshima, I saw Keijiro, and every year I had to reintroduce myself. His health was fading with each visit, as was his memory. He had battled liver cancer and blood disease for years. He would never say for certain whether he attributed them to the atomic bomb,

but he guessed that they probably were a result of his exposure. But he carried on and remained active at the Hiroshima Peace Memorial Museum as a volunteer.

While in the backseat on the four-hour drive to Baltimore from New York City on Thanksgiving 2014, I Googled Keijiro to see if he was up to anything. I looked in the news section. The first headline read, "Hiroshima Survivor, Nuclear Critic Keijiro Matsushima Dies." There are few hibakusha left in the world, and even fewer who can speak English. The weight of the words heard directly from witnesses of atomic weaponry is 100 percent more powerful from their mouths alone. No one will ever hear him tell his story again.

I was a sixteen-year-old student of the technical college in the city. While most of the students had evacuated or been put to work, we were learning math on the morning of August 6. Our school was located about two kilometers from the hypocenter in a neighborhood called Senda-machi. My classroom was located on the second floor of a two-story wooden building. There were seventeen boys in that room. It was a big room, and I sat next to the window on the south side. Fortunately, our school started at eight o'clock. As you know, the bomb dropped at eight fifteen. If school had started at eight thirty, we would have been incinerated in the streetcars.

I looked out of the south window and saw two B-29s. The *Enola Gay* might have already dropped the bomb and escaped. The B-29s glimmered in the atmosphere over ten thousand meters above. Japan didn't have any more fighter planes or any antiaircraft guns to fight back with. American planes were flying freely.

Only a moment later, the explosion went off. A very strong flash erupted in my eyes. From over a mile away, I could feel the heat. I covered my ears and eyes and jumped under the desk. The noise of one hundred thunders followed.

My school collapsed, and everything became dark, pitch black, and very quiet. All of my classmates were there, but no one screamed. I guess that everyone was busy taking care of themselves. No sound, no voices—it was deadly quiet in a dark world. Real hell.

I crawled around on the floor, my whole body bleeding from head to toe. My shirt and pants were torn. I thought I would be killed at any minute. *Help me, Buddha. Help, Mother.* I thought maybe one or two minutes later, the whole ceiling would fall on us. The center of our room caved in, but the area around me was OK. The floor was still intact, and I was close to a door. I was cut, I noticed, from small pieces of the windowpane. I crept out of the building. The staircase was warped but still walkable. I thought a bomb must have been dropped right outside. When I emerged, I was surprised to see the entire city turned into an inferno; the whole neighborhood was demolished.

I only saw two bombers. What could they have done? We had no idea about such a big bomb. Students appeared out of the darkness, made visible by the flames of their burning schools. Everyone was wounded with no exceptions—men, women, children, horses—all of them bleeding, bearing broken bones, with debris protruding from them from wherever the shockwave hit.

I heard one of my friends cry for help. Seeing a big cut on his head, I thought of taking him to the Red Cross hospital about a few hundred feet north of our school. We walked out of the school gate and were shocked at how all of the houses were destroyed, with roof tiles and debris scattered everywhere. The streetcars were stopped here and there; electric poles were down, their wires dangling, and the whole city was on fire. Clouds of smoke whirled in the streets. Above all, we were shocked to see hundreds of people coming from the central area in a long line to the south.

Along the streetcar railroad was a procession of people. Their hair either stood up or had fallen out. Some were burned to the bone. Some were burned head to feet, char-coal-gray skin peeling from their faces, necks, breasts, and arms. Some of their arms had swollen to look like pigs, and under their peeled skin, I could see red muscle. Of course, their clothes had torn and singed off. Some of them were almost naked, leaving just some clothes around their waists. They held out their arms because of the pain. It was a long line from the central area, with hundreds of survivors. *Why are they so badly burned? Did they drop thousands of firebombs at once?* I wondered.

The front yard of the Red Cross hospital was full of the wounded and the burned. Doctors and nurses were wounded, too. Only one doctor and a pair of nurses, frantic with the very little medicine they had, were attending to the injured.

I thought that we would have to wait for a long time. I was not sure if they could give sufficient treatment for my friend. "There's no help around here. Let's go back to the school," I said to my injured friend.

When we went back near the school, an army rescue truck came across Miyuki-bashi Bridge. This one might have been the first rescue vehicle from the army transportation corps stationing in Ujina harbor district, and my friend was really lucky to get on this car then. Later, I learned that he was sent to Ninoshima Island, which is about two kilometers from the harbor, and survived his injuries. [1]

I couldn't reach the center of the city. I saw many people who couldn't walk, who crawled to the riversides, begged for water, and drowned in the rivers. Piles of bodies lined the streets. Weakened and flammable Japanese houses were consumed by the firestorm. People had to run away, leaving their loved ones buried under the smashed houses. Kids who were not burned, not even injured, were stuck.

"Run away!"

"Leave me here!"

---

1   The outcome of his friend's survival was revealed in Matsushima-san's public testimony "The A-Bomb That I Experienced," hosted online at Hiroshima World Friendship Center's website.

"Fire is coming!" the kids yelled to their parents. While I was bleeding a lot from the small cuts caused by the window and debris, my bones were OK. My injuries were not so serious. In many ways, I was one of the fortunate ones.

When I crossed Miyuki-bashi Bridge, I could see both sides of the river burning. *Hiroshima is destroyed. America must have invented such a big bomb. Goddamn it, it's going to be difficult to win this war.* I remembered an article in a boys' magazine from a couple of years before. The article had said a small bomb the size of a matchbox could destroy a warship. The name of it was an atomic bomb.

On that day, I didn't believe in surrender. I walked and walked. Hiroshima Station was on fire. Trains had already stopped. I had to walk many miles, but by nightfall, I reached my mother's home in the farm country. Those days, my mother was my only family: my brothers were at war, and my father had already died from illness.

The next day, I became very ill. I had a high fever and diarrhea, which must have been immediate aftereffects of radiation. But I was still young and able to recover after a week or ten days. Even today, I suffer from the effects, but I am still alive. In my case, only two kilometers away from the hypocenter, I must have been exposed to a lot of radiation.

I left Hiroshima very soon after, which was for the best. A lot of people who were not bombed in Hiroshima, rescue workers and those looking for their relatives, came into the city the next day. They stayed a couple of days or longer and were affected by radiation. After they got home, some of them fell ill and died. We had no knowledge of radiation back then. Again, I was very lucky, as a lot of people around me died one by one.

Healthy-looking people with no injuries and no burns suddenly became ill with strange symptoms. They developed high fevers, lost their hair, bled from their gums, and grew many spots. We called it the A-bomb disease. Doctors didn't know anything about radioactivity, and most of the people who suffered from those symptoms died.

Very soon after the bomb, we became good friends with the American forces who came in. To blame each other today doesn't make any sense. An argument about such things is fruitless. If we Japanese blame the United States for Hiroshima and Nagasaki, Americans might want to say, "What about Pearl Harbor or the march in Bataan?" and the two sides will blame each other. It makes no sense.

The majority of Americans believe that Fat Man and Little Boy were necessary to end the war sooner. It was really meaningful to them to save more lives of American soldiers—and also Japanese lives that would have been lost in a drawn out invasion. This kind of logic makes some sense, but we citizens of Hiroshima just want America to know what the horrible reality of the atomic bomb was. We just want Americans to know that and to cooperate and have a common opinion opposing nukes from now on for the peaceful future of the world.

* * *

12

WELCOME TO THE PROJECT

1944

It was as picturesque a morning as the Wendover base could have, though nothing about the flat land and the brown mountains seemed beautiful to Lt. Beser. He didn't have time to pay attention to the puffy clouds that floated into the endless blue sky or the faraway mountain ranges that surrounded the base.

Why was I the only one called out? He didn't have much time to think. He had only fifteen minutes to shower and dress. He swiftly changed into his nicest uniform and was still tucking it in several blocks from the headquarters, imagining what, exactly, his new commanding officer wanted. *If you can, you will,* he thought, *and if you can't, just say so. But what makes you so sure you're going to be asked to do something? Maybe you already did something. Maybe you're going to be invited to leave.*

When he entered Col. Tibbets's office, he immediately realized he had been called for some type of interview. The desk was pushed back, and representatives of the army, air force, and navy, along with some civilian scientists, occupied a semicircle of chairs. For over an hour, Dr. Hal Brode, a professor from the University of California, fired questions at him about his various technical trainings and the marks he had earned.

Near the end of the interview, Dr. Brode asked Jake skeptically, "How do you feel about flying combat?"

"I've never had any combat experience," he admitted, "but I have been thoroughly trained for it."

Brode broke from his poker face momentarily and chaffed, "Well, it's not that we don't already have people for the job for which we are considering you, but our people are just too valuable to risk."

Jake just shrugged his shoulders and watched his life expectancy sink and his insurance premium skyrocket. He was excused from the room, and about ten minutes later, he was called back in. When he reentered, Commander Ashworth was already on the phone talking to someone, saying, "I'll bring him up there as soon as possible."

Everyone else congratulated him for just having been picked for "the team." As Ashworth hung up the phone, he reassured the now-anxious lieutenant, "Don't worry. I'm going to take you to meet some more Project people, and you'll get a better idea of what's going on." He noticed Jake looked confused. Taking note, Ashworth chuckled and said, "Welcome to the Project."

*   *   *

13

Shoso Kawamoto, Ten Years Old

It had been ten years since the Hiroshima bomb. Of the eighty-six hundred students who evacuated, about six thousand of them went to live with families and relatives outside Hiroshima. About twenty-six hundred had no one and lived on the streets, alone in the city. Eventually, orphanages accepted about six hundred of them. About two thousand of them were still living on the streets. Yakuza gangs came from other cities and promised to help rebuild. Those who could get jobs with them were taken care of. About one thousand street kids became gangsters this way.

Shoso Kawamoto tried to join up but was rejected as "too gentle." He saw friend after friend disappear to cruel fates, forgotten. Fifty years after the dropping of the bomb, he came back for a reunion and to visit the Peace Memorial Museum. The museum showed countless photos of people who had been radiated or burned. When it came to photos of the orphans who had survived, though, there was one picture of a shoe-shining boy, but it didn't have any description or information about his story, except for a sign that read, "All orphaned children were categorized as 'missing.' Kawamoto-san knew some had survived. He had survived, yet they were considered "missing." He became upset enough that he started talking about his experience. That's why he joined the museum, becoming a Hiroshima Peace volunteer, and he's been talking ever since.

There were nine of us in my family: my parents, my six siblings, and me. My dad was in the navy for about ten years, and he received a pension for his tenure of service. My mother's father was working for the last of the Asano clan. My mom probably had about six siblings herself and was the youngest of them, born in the *hino-uma*, the year of the horse. My dad was from a rural farming family, so he wouldn't normally have been able to marry somebody of my mother's status. However, because he was getting a pension from the military and because it was the wish of my mother's father to get her married off as soon as possible, her father allowed the marriage.

My mom came from a good family who raised her strictly, and thus she was strict with me. For instance, she would say, "Boys should not show their teeth. They should not smile." But my dad was a farmer, so he was not interested in that kind of education. He was, however, a really hard worker. We were an unbalanced family in that respect.

But my mom's stringent methods really paid off for me in the long run. "You are a child who can achieve anything you want if only you try. If you do not succeed, it's because you didn't try," she used to say.

In most families, the father was the most important figure, and women/mothers usually obeyed him. My mother built our family by taking good care of and respecting our father. She never bought things for herself. Instead, she made sure that my dad had plenty. Dad liked liquor and cigarettes, so she made sure to never run out of those. So even though my dad didn't have much of an education because he was a farmer, my mom took very good care of him. That was the Japanese way.

Education for boys was serious. My mom thought that girls needed to learn how to sew and cook, but she wanted to make sure we boys studied hard. She wore makeup only on New Year's and Obon, the holiday when Japanese Buddhists greet our ancestral spirits. So she wore makeup only two days a year, and I remember well how happy it made me feel to see her look so beautiful.

The Sino-Japanese War had started, and Japanese people experienced numerous supply shortages. But I remember still receiving pink-and-white rice cakes in elementary school until classes ceased.

After we entered elementary school, we stopped playing with our toys, which included *takeuma* (stilts made of bamboo) and *kamideppo* (paper guns). Instead, we played sports like triangle baseball. Unlike today's baseball diamonds, we saved space by playing in a triangle with two bases.

Also, we started to learn how to make airplanes. We would sharpen bamboo and then use candles to heat it and bend it to make wings. But eventually, we no longer had the materials, so my mother taught us how to fold airplanes from paper. We took postcards, bent them in half, and folded as many as we could.

In 1944, the war intensified; American air raids became more frequent. Hiroshima City had thirty-six elementary schools. We heard the stories about how badly Tokyo and Nagoya were being destroyed. Kyushu was not damaged yet, but the destruction started to spread in September.

Streets back then were very narrow. We didn't have the ten- and twenty-ton trucks like today. The biggest trucks were about four tons. Also, very few families had cars. Most families had a wagon or cart, or maybe a bicycle. So there was no use for large, wide streets. When American bombs were dropped on these narrow roads, then, the damage was huge.

Children were among those evacuating by way of these streets, and that slowed down the crowd a lot. As a strategy for minimizing damage and allowing quicker travel, it was decided that we should widen the streets. So starting in November, we had to take down the houses on both sides of the streets and widen the roads. This required forced evacuation of the hundreds of thousands of people whose homes stood in the way.

Eventually, most of the families in Hiroshima started sending their children to rural towns to evacuate them, too, in case of attack. I was ten, in the sixth grade, when the rural evacuations started. They were going to evacuate all kids from first grade through sixth grade (elementary school years), but then they decided first-and second-graders still needed their parents, so those kids stayed behind.

At that time, there were roughly six thousand first- and second-graders from the thirty-six elementary schools. These kids stayed in Hiroshima. Eighty-six hundred students from third through sixth grade evacuated approximately fifty kilometers or more away. I think it couldn't be helped. We had heard about the bombings in Tokyo and Osaka. Kids were becoming a burden, and many lives were being lost in the air raids. So the military forced the student evacuations. When the parents in Hiroshima heard all this, they assumed they should do the same, though no official order was sent out immediately.

The evacuations started in April 1945. The buildings were still coming down. The farmers and village folks took care of the students. We lived in temples and were divided into groups of forty to fifty kids each. My group slept in the main hall with the Buddha statue. We laid down our futons in rows and put up the mosquito nets when the spring turned into summer.

There wasn't really a ration of rice back then, but since we were evacuated to the farm area, we didn't have much. We each had about 250 grams of rice a day mixed with wheat and soy, along with potatoes and sweet potatoes. We had one bowl per kid. For sides, we had daikon radishes, burdock, and, if there was meat, frog. Of course we were hungry. We ate our lunches as soon as we arrived at school, so we wouldn't have any food left by lunchtime. Then, we would try to convince the farmers' kids to share their food by trading them pencils and crayons. Since we were city kids, we had things like stationery, so we would trade it for food from the farmer kids.

There weren't any real studies. For half of the "study day," we would cultivate the land and grow potatoes and vegetables. We would slice cuts into pine trees, put bamboo cups under the cuts, and collect the pine resin. One day when I was out on collecting duty, I noticed a white cloud rising in the direction of Hiroshima.

My youngest sister was in first grade, and my brother was four years old, so they had not evacuated. My father and my second-oldest sister were out working on broadening the streets. Because my oldest sister survived, she and I were able to stay in a room inside Hiroshima Station for six months. She worked in the management office, which was adjacent to where we were living.

At the time, I had relatives alive. But they started saying that they were going to separate my sister and me. My dad's side of the family was going to take my sister, and my mom's side of the family was going to take me. This made my sister upset, and she said we were the only ones who had survived and would not be separated. That's why we lived in a room. It was burned in the fire, but everybody at her work loved her, so we were able to get this room. Because it was inside a station, there was a bathroom with plumbing and a sink, so we could live there.

However, six months later, my sister died of leukemia. My uncle from my dad's side came and took me, but he wasn't interested in actually keeping me, so right away he tried to put me in an orphanage. But it had already been almost a year since the bombing, and the facilities and system were full. It embarrassed me to hear my uncle argue about what to do. A village mayor by the name of Kawanaka-san overheard the situation and took me in.

I was eleven years old then and still in sixth grade. Mr. Kawanaka was really good to me. I worked at his factory for ten years. When I was a little over twenty, he built me a house.

"It's time to get married!" he said, but when I went to the house where the girl I liked lived, the family refused.

"You are from Hiroshima of that time. You probably have radiation contamination. If our daughter marries you, she will have children with defects."

I had my own house, but it didn't matter. *That's it. I'm never going to rely on anybody again. I'm going to live alone.* I ran away from Kawanaka-san's house and went back to Hiroshima.

In Hiroshima a month after the bomb, a large typhoon called Makurazaki came through and swept away the radiation. So it was possible to live in Hiroshima again. However, no supplies came from anywhere. For ten years, most of Hiroshima City was abandoned. After the typhoon swept away the radiation, the farmers' wives from the surrounding areas came together to cook potato porridge for the approximately two thousand kids still living on the streets. But they made enough for only about six hundred kids.

All the older kids, who were nine or ten, would stick their hands out first and get the food, so there wasn't any left when the seven- and eight-year-olds' turns came. The ladies would add more water, but there wasn't enough. At the end, they would wash the pots with water and soak that water into handkerchiefs, which the kids would suck on. As we approached December, even the handkerchiefs stopped coming. When it was all over, about one thousand kids died of hunger and cold.

I was living with my sister in the train station until about February, so I witnessed all of this. The kids who died would have pebbles in their mouths because they had tried to suck water out of them. Back then, all the kids who died would be carried away in the river.

In those days, they just categorized everybody as "missing." The kids who survived the atomic bomb but were not able to live afterward were called "missing" in the history books.

Everybody from this generation left school in the middle of their elementary years, so none of them could actually get jobs in the markets and companies because nobody would vouch for them. The only option they had was to work for the yakuza gang. The little kids mostly died. I knew of about two hundred girls who had been sold away by the gang. But there was nothing that could be done. Kids who were adopted mostly got through middle school and some high school. Those who were not adopted were allowed to take an exam to become a public official. Those kids were able to join the police reserve force, our current self-defense force. For the rest, nothing could be done.

This is the Hiroshima I came back to when I was twenty. These kids had barely survived for the last ten years. They considered everybody around them an enemy, and nobody was going to help them. If anybody had food, they had stolen it. If one of them had survived, it meant he or she had done something violent to sustain themselves. I would run into some of my pals from back then ten years later, and they had grown into gang leaders themselves. Even some of them who had evacuated with their relatives got involved because the job market was so poor. Everybody was an enemy.

I had given up at that time. I had a driver's license, so I was always able to get a job and get paid, but really nobody wanted to help. There were no allies. People needed to find their own paths in life.

I tried to join the yakuza myself. I would gamble and fight. They rejected me, though. They said, "It's not your path, Shoso. You're too kind to become a yakuza."

Maybe they were right. Those very friends got themselves killed.

Around the same time I tried to join the gangs, I had my license revoked because of an infraction. I decided to take my own life. But I didn't want to die in Hiroshima. My family had all been killed there. Now the gangs ruled the streets, and I would have been thrown away like a piece of trash in the city that my family was buried in.

I went to Okayama and found an udon (noodle) shop in the city center. They were hiring. I realized nobody knew me in Okayama. Instead of killing myself, I decided to re-start my life. I started working there and would labor diligently in the food-service industry for thirty years. After three years, I was able to get a job at the employee cafeteria at Tenmaya (a department store). That's when I met my culinary friends, and the five of us created a bento business.

I swore off love and never got married. And when we all turned fifty, we went our separate ways and built our own independent food shops. My company would employ between forty and fifty people.

When I was sixty, I got a phone call from one of my friends with whom I had evacuated. He invited me to go back to Hiroshima for the fiftieth anniversary memorial service. That's why I came back. It was on August 6.

I visited the Peace Memorial Park when I was there. Ten years later, I moved back and started volunteering. In the park, there is the peace bell. The map of the world wraps around it, but it has no national boundaries.

In order for the children of today to create a world without boundaries, the seniors of today need to persistently tell the stories of the past. How are we going to create this new world and not repeat the mistakes? How can the kids of tomorrow find ways to overcome their differences and build a better future? We can't continue to blame one another about the past.

*　　*　　*

14

GOING TO BE A WEAPON

1944

With an absence of records due to a fire in the Saint Louis archives facility, Beser thinks he was ordered to the flight line sometime around the first week of October or the last week of September, about three weeks after his roundtable interview. He was told to pack for a three-day trip—winter uniform. Upon arriving at the flight line at 0730 hours, Col. Tibbets and Commander Ashworth were waiting with several civilians and their pilot of the designated aircraft, a C-47 transport vessel.

Jake was preparing to join everyone on the airplane when a civilian grabbed him. He was a gumshoe, a security man, and he took all of Jake's air-force insignia from him. "Put these castles on," he said. The gold castle is the symbol of the US Army Corps of Engineers.

Beser found it peculiar, but he noticed Col. Tibbets also undergoing an insignia change and thought no further of it. Beser entered the transport carrier and was greeted by an old friend. And on this day, Art Henderson didn't have a copilot. Beser had flown with Art countless times in Florida. "Get in the right seat for me, Jake."

"Like old times? Sure thing, Art. Where we going?" asked Beser.

Art, who seemed used to the world of top secret, said, "I'm not sure. They'll tell me when I take off."

They started to roll into takeoff, and as they broke ground and Jake brought up the landing gear, Art noticed Beser's new castles. "Hey, I thought you were in the air force."

"I was until I got on this plane," retorted Beser, just as confused as his friend—except his friend *wasn't* confused. Beser later found out that part of "the game" was to see if he could keep his mouth shut, and Art had been ordered to ask questions and judge his responses. When they cleared the runway, Wendover Tower directed them toward site Y and then furnished more directions when they reached the air over Salt Lake City.

Having been there before, Art said, "We're probably going to Santa Fe. When we get there, there's going to be a car waiting for us to take us to Los Alamos."

About an hour later, the plane was instructed to land in Santa Fe. Sure enough, a staff car was already waiting in the practically unused civilian airport. At that point, Commander Ashworth announced, "We're going to Los Alamos Ranch Boys' School."

Los Alamos Ranch School was located on a mesa forty minutes outside of Santa Fe. The US military must have selected this location because of its remoteness from civilization and its abundance of unused real estate. When Beser arrived, he saw an awesome sight: instead of hills covered with sheep, there lay a brand-new city, as if Rome really were built in a day. The school had been transformed into an industrial compound with all the trappings of an army base. And he thought, *My God, what's going on here?* The most brilliant minds in the world gathered there, half of them scheming to unlock the power of the sun and the other half to turn it into a weapon. Jake was a member of the latter category.

"Welcome to Location Y," said Tibbets, the man who knew its secrets.

Beser still did not know what awaited him in the classrooms of this old school once attended by the director of Location Y, Robert Oppenheimer. He assumed his new job would be something related to radar because that's where his qualifications stood, but he had no idea what it would be until he was introduced to Dr. Norman Ramsey. Formerly of Columbia University, Ramsey had become a director of Project Alberta, the fusing and firing section of the Manhattan District.

Before Ramsey could begin explaining what Project Alberta, or Project A, was, he was paged over the public-address system. Commander Ashworth realized at once that he was supposed to have taken Beser to the security office for a briefing before any of this started.

Ashworth accompanied Beser, offered apologetic explanations to the security officer as to why they had not appeared there first, and reassured him that the new recruit still didn't know anything.

"As of the moment, Lieutenant, other than making him aware of the existence of this place, we have not yet disclosed any of the details of the mission to him. Frankly speaking, he doesn't know jack shit."

"General, this is an oversight that cannot be repeated. Do I need to make myself any more clear? Do you understand what is at stake here?"

Ashworth nodded.

"*Do you?*" pressed the second lieutenant security officer, trying hard to emphasize the seriousness without saying much.

"Yes, Lieutenant," said Ashworth, noticeably frustrated with the patronizing officer.

Ramsey and company proceeded to instruct Beser on the ins and outs of handling any information he might receive. "Lieutenant, I cannot stress enough the importance of not letting on to the people outside of the technical area that you are in the air force. That would make clear the nature of the device. Our scientists can't know that what they are making is going to be a weapon."

*　　*　　*

15

MASAHIRO SASAKI, FOUR YEARS OLD

Two weeks before his new documentary was to screen in Shibuya, Tokyo, Shinpei Takeda received a strange request: his friend at the Asahi Shimbun wanted him to meet a young American with a unique connection to both sides of the atomic bomb. It was my second week in Japan, and I needed all the help I could get, so I enlisted the reporter who had interviewed me in the article that had started this journey. Beyond inviting me to take part in a Q and A at his movie screening, he knew the exact person to introduce me to, Yuji Sasaki. Yuji was the nephew of Sadako Sasaki, the girl who died folding paper cranes, tried to cure her leukemia with modern medicine and a traditional Japanese legend. The legend says that if you fold one thousand cranes, you can receive a wish. She didn't receive that wish, but her friends and family carried on her spirit and erected a statue in her honor.

Shinpei met me at Nakano Station. We wandered through the windy alleyways full of bustling pachinko clubs, izakaya pubs, Lawsons, and 7-Elevens. Finally, we took a turn and reached a quiet street with a ramen flag in front of a small, garage-sized noodle shop as quiet as the alley outside. The only host, an attractive young man with a pink shirt, an apron, and cowboy boots, smiled and greeted me, introducing himself as Yuji.

"Two years ago, my father, Masahiro, met the grandson of President Truman when we donated one of Sadako's cranes to the 9/11 Memorial, and he asked him to work with us to send a message of peace." He stopped talking and ran back into his kitchen to pull out a tiny white box. Inside was a paper crane the size of a dime and a paper triangle that could have made a crane the same size. "This is Sadako's last crane, and this is the crane she didn't finish." He held out my hand and put the crane in my palm. "Tiny, isn't it?" He paused, giving me a moment to take in the gravity of what I was holding, and then asked, "Ari, will you work with Sadako Legacy and send a message of peace?" I told him I would do what I could. Sadako Legacy believes in the power of human connection and the power of good intention. They have sent Sadako's actual cranes around the world to places they think that need them. Now Sadako's cranes rest in the Arizona Memorial, where a Pearl Harbor survivor exclaimed, "They say you can't teach an old dog new tricks!" Inspired by the gift, he got up out

of his wheelchair and hugged Yuji's father, Masahiro, to prove everyone wrong.

My first memory that I have is playing with Sadako. I was four, and she was two. We were playing near my house when I took off all of my clothes and left them in the road. The toddler picked up my clothes, folded them, and took them back home. Sadako used to act like the older sibling. That's how we grew up. There were air raids, and Sadako took my hands and led me to the shelter when I should have led her.

One of a four-year-old's first memories shouldn't be an atomic bomb. Even so, I never had a bad impression of America. Soldiers came in and gave us chocolates after the war. I might have been more hateful if I had been injured, but miraculously I escaped unharmed, unlike my sister.

Sadako was taken to the ABCC (Atomic Bomb Casualty Commission) every year and examined but never treated. Each year she went in, and each year she was cleared of the so-called A-bomb disease. For a time, our family was happy. My father opened a barbershop in a good area of the city, and life was good...for a time.

On February 21, 1950, Sadako was hospitalized with swollen glands. My father had her checked out at the ABCC, and they recommended her to hospital after hospital, the biggest in Hiroshima. From January to February, she was tested, until she was finally admitted to the Atomic Bomb Hospital, present-day Niseki Hospital.

For our family, it seemed everything collapsed at once. My father became the guarantor for his friend. Then, the man ran out of town in the middle of the night and left our family in debt. Father was trusting and kind and knew that his friend was in trouble, but he didn't expect him to leave him cold. When Sadako was hospitalized, we didn't have money for a kimono. Father had to borrow one from relatives. When he took her to the finest kimono shop in Hiroshima, Sadako begged him, "Please don't buy something so nice for me." Sadako knew we didn't have any money, but Father insisted.

How did Sadako become the girl who folded the paper cranes? She let out both the pain of our parents and her own suffering with each crane. She hid her suffering and was very tolerant of the pain. She didn't want anyone to worry. She didn't complain to her friends or to us. Her spirit encouraged others around her to speak of her bravery.

She became famous for her hospital manner. She behaved normally and never said the word *pain*. Leukemia is a cancer, and the treatment is excruciating, but she never uttered a complaint in front of our parents or me. She never asked for any painkillers because she knew we couldn't afford them. If it were me, I wouldn't have been able to stand the pain, but I'm not Sadako.

One summer night, she broke her strong character. I think she was beginning to accept her fate. We went up to the roof of the hospital and stared out at the clear night sky over the flat plane that was being reconstructed back into Hiroshima. "Brother, if we pass away, do you think we become a star?"

I didn't know what to say. I had never seen that side of her before. "How have you been so tolerant?" I asked her.

"Because of the cranes," she said, staring into the stars. "When I make paper cranes, I focus on them. One is a prayer for life, one is a prayer for peace, one is a prayer for Mom and Dad, and one is a prayer for you."

She reached one thousand cranes and was on her way to her second thousand. But her body became weak, and the paper ornaments grew smaller and smaller. As her condition worsened, the cranes became more difficult for her to fold. However, there wasn't a single clumsy paper crane. Each was perfect.

I heard from people that, when Robert Jungk came to Hiroshima, he heard about Sadako. There was already a statue for her that her classmates raised money to build. Robert Jungk introduced Sadako to the world, Karl Bruckner wrote a book about her, and Ellen La Coeur translated it into English.

In the book, Bruckner wrote that she folded roughly six hundred cranes. It made a nice story that she didn't reach the fabled number to get a wish, but it wasn't true. She was trying to make one thousand more when she died.

Not everybody was happy that Sadako's story was told worldwide. It got back to my parents that people were speaking badly about our family, saying we profited from

Sadako's story. We didn't. This was the biggest reason we never wanted to tell the story of Sadako in Hiroshima. Everyone in Hiroshima had a Sadako, only none of those children stood on top of that statue; it was the Sasakis' child.

We left Hiroshima and moved to Kyushu, where we had relatives. In 2009, we started donating her remaining cranes around the world to places that needed a symbol of peace. We sent one to the 9/11 Memorial. After the tsunami on March 11, 2011, we sent a paper crane folded from debris of the World Trade Center as a monument to the Fukushima city of Koriama. We want to spread a message of peace and human connection.

*   *   *

Above photos from left to right, Sadako's
last crane and the crane she didn't fininsh.
Yuji Sadako's nephew visits Nagasaki in 2012.
Photos of Sadako and family courtesy
of the Sasaki Family.

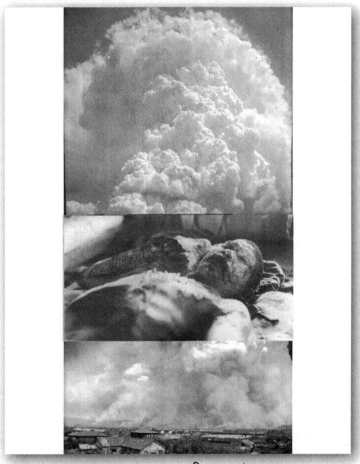

Photos courtesy of the Hiroshima
Peace Memorial Museum

Photos by Orval Eli Labig

16

GIVE 'EM HELL, JAKE

1945

Once Beser's security briefing was complete, the members of Project A went back to Ramsey's office, and he began to address some of the problems he had in his group. He gave Beser a more thorough briefing as to what was expected of him. At no time did he come right out and say they were trying to build an atomic bomb, but he used phrases like "fundamental forces being released" and "chain reactions taking place," causing a "light hotter than one thousand suns." The assumption was, if Beser had enough brains and stayed there long enough, he would figure it out. By the end of the first day, he knew exactly what was going on.

What was immediately apparent was that they had a bomb, and they had initiators for the bomb fairly well developed, but they needed something that would set the thing off at a given height above the ground. It had to be variable, whereby the topographic geography of the target city would be fed into their calculations, and they would decide how high above the ground it needed to go off. Beser didn't think that sounded like much of a problem at all, and remembering the tech orders in his briefcase, he asked, "Does anyone have a Sig-Five catalog?"

"No. What's a Sig-Five?" asked Ramsey.

"It's a stock catalog of the Signal Corps. It lists everything in production. It comes out every month. I'm sure they have it over at the base signal office."

Ramsey sent an assistant over, and half an hour later, he came back with a big telephone-directory-type book. Beser sifted through the pages until he found what he was looking for.

"See this?" He pointed at the page. "It's an AN/APS-Thirteen, a tail warning radar that we built for the B-17s and B-24s flying over Europe to alert pilots that someone's on their tail. It has a variable range gate. It rings a bell and flashes a light in the cockpit to warn the pilot that there's something in his lethal range. This thing will fit where you want it to fit. You don't have to reinvent the wheel like you've been trying to do. Not only that, but I have the tech order in my briefcase."

Ramsey invited everyone besides Beser to leave the room.

Over the next two to three hours, they went through the ins and outs of the equipment and redesigned the fuse of the "gimmick." Ramsey got on the telephone and called in the appropriate code to Dayton, Ohio, for those people to get up to Camden, New Jersey; get twenty boxes off the production line; and get those boxes to Dayton immediately.

Beser and Art flew through the night to Dayton, Ohio. They got there at 5:00 a.m., took showers, drank black coffee while they loaded up the airplane, regassed it, and turned right around and went back to Los Alamos with twenty radar sets in tow. From that point on, it was a matter of modifying them slightly, giving them some jamming immunity from other disturbances. They installed one of them in a trainer-type aircraft in a twin-engine Beech, flew profiles where they came in at fairly steep angles, and, as they got into the desired altitude over the ground, made sure the lights came on and the bells rang. The members of Project A realized that this thing would work like a charm, except that they needed a better antenna—a better radiator to put on the bomb shade. In less than an hour, they had designed an antenna, and they built it in less than a week.

Beser worked with Mr. Lem Skaggs at Location Y, and Dr. Edward Doll would come to Wendover periodically with tasks. Beser needed to become thoroughly familiar with the electronic fuse and all of its idiosyncrasies. It would be his responsibility to see that nothing interfered with its proper operation over the target. He was also told that he would fly with each one of the fuses until such a time that the medics said he had enough. No one knew at that time how many of the gimmicks were planned for use.

Precautions were taken to disguise Beser's military affiliation, but they were not enough. On the second night of his visit to Location Y, he went to the post exchange (PX) with Mr. Sheldon Dike, a fellow engineer who at one time worked for the Martin Company in Baltimore. While standing at the counter waiting for a beer, a member of the Women's Army Auxiliary Corps (WAAC) standing alongside them whispered to her friend, "That little fellow is wearing a 'forty-mission hat' if ever I've seen one."

In the attempt to disguise his service affiliation, a change of hat was overlooked. Needless to say, they left the PX at once and returned to the guest lodge where Beser was staying. After he told the story to Ashworth, he was assigned an escort whenever he left Wendover, except for the times he traveled with Col. Tibbets.

Col. Tibbets still made periodic trips to the Pentagon, and on one such visit, Beser went along with him. The final decision on the employment of radar was under review.

Ashworth tipped off Beser that radar was not being considered as a primary bombing aid if the target was obscured by weather. This bothered him, as his crew had been subjected to a fair number of radar drops in their training program, and of course he had developed a larger parochial interest.

Col. Tibbets introduced him to the group in attendance as his radar officer, and he was seated next to Col. Stuart "Stud" Wright, whom Beser had known since his days at Boca Raton and who had gained a tremendous reputation in the South Pacific for the job that he and his radar-equipped Liberator bombers had done on the Japanese.

When the group arrived it had been made apparent that the decision not to allow the use of radar as the primary bombing aid had been cast in concrete. The topic of discussion in this meeting was the use of radio navigation beams laid down from submarines hovering off the coast of Japan. Beser turned to Col. Wright and said, "Bullshit" scoffing at the unrealistic plan.

The colonel replied," Give 'em Hell Jake.

*   *   *

17

HIROYUKI GOTO, SEVENTEEN YEARS OLD

One night, Goto woke up out of his sleep. An artist, he had walls covered with his watercolor sketches. He had to transfer the images from his dreams onto paper. By the time he was done, he had eight panels. In the sixty-seven years since he had survived the atomic destruction of Hiroshima, he had never drawn what he saw that day. The next week, he would be meeting the eldest grandson of President Harry S. Truman and the grandson of Jacob Beser, together. It was all arranged by Sadako Legacy, and Yuji, an old family friend, would facilitate the meeting. Goto didn't blame Clifton or me. He remembered training to kill US combat men with bamboo sticks. He was prepared to die. He was seventeen years old. You can look at Japan's wartime condition in one of two ways: they were so desperate to win the war, their thirteen-year-olds were ready to fight, or else they were so desperate that they were down to their thirteen-year-olds to fight.

*   *   *

Courtesy of the Hiroshima
Peace Memorial Museum

August 6, 1945, 8:15 a.m. After the morning assembly at Hiroshima Communication School.

Courtesy of the Hiroshima
Peace Memorial Museum

August 6, 1945. If I had stayed where I was five minutes before the atomic bomb dropped, I would have had broken glass stuck all over my body.

Courtesy of the Hiroshima
Peace Memorial Museum

August 7, 1945. A man with bandages on his head, bleeding and looking like a police officer, gave out disaster certificates at the West Miyuki Bridge.

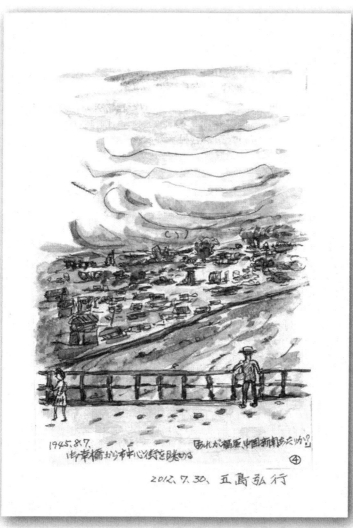

Courtesy of the Hiroshima
Peace Memorial Museum

August 7, 1945. Looking out at the downtown area from Miyuki Bridge, I wondered, Is that where the Fukuya department store and Chugoku Shimbun newspaper were?

Courtesy of the Hiroshima
Peace Memorial Museum

August 7, 1945. At the Takano Bridge, everyone wanted "water!"

Courtesy of the Hiroshima
Peace Memorial Museum

August 7, 1945. Near the Takano Bridge, Japanese marines known as the Akatsuki Corps threw bodies on the back of a truck.

Courtesy of the Hiroshima
Peace Memorial Museum

August 7, 1945. This was a triage center. You can see the armbands of the Otake neighborhood support group and the Hatsukaichi neighborhood support groups.

Courtesy of the Hiroshima
Peace Memorial Museum

August 7, 1945. On the stairs near the Meiji Bridge, when I went to put my hands on this boy's shoulder to check if he was OK, his body fell over. He was already dead. I could only pray.

18

THE RUMORS BEGAN TO FLY

1945

Gen. Groves, presiding over the meeting, looked at Beser dead-on and asked, "What did you say, lieutenant?"

"Bullshit," he repeated calmly. Beser saw Col. Tibbets out of the corner of his eye, looking as if he wanted the floor to swallow him up. "That's a terrible idea. It won't work!" continued the outspoken lieutenant.

"Why do you say that?" Groves, not about to let a first lieutenant show him up, tried to keep his calm.

"Can I come down to the blackboard?" asked Beser.

"You certainly may."

"The radius plus the angle error at the end of the radius is a function of the stability of the center. I don't believe you can hold a submarine that steady. The tides are going to pull it off track. The boat's gonna be fighting the motion of the sea. The submarine must be on the surface for it to work. And in no way can it remain surfaced three miles off the Japanese coast without coming under attack."

"Those reasons seem fair enough," said Groves simply, and they moved on.

Beser did not win his case then and there because they were not about to reward this lieutenant for making an ass out of the general.

The days at Wendover turned into weeks, and the weeks turned into months. New people came; some stayed, and some went. Gradually, the 393rd became the unit that would eventually go overseas with the "gimmick." Jimmy Galbreath had the communications section, Elroy Homa the radar section, and Jacob Beser the radar countermeasures section. Each was responsible for the training of his assigned personnel. Eventually, being the senior electronics officer in the squadron, Beser was assigned overall surveillance of this activity. A group radar officer was supposed to assist and supervise him, but if that officer ever did his job, Beser was never aware of it. The fellows in both the radar and the countermeasures sections shared a common workshop, and the noncoms knew their job very well. It is a well-known fact of life in the service that without the sergeants, nothing happens. Their sergeants, Wendell Lathrop and Porter Richardson, knew their jobs and knew exactly how to handle their men. The squadron's excellent maintenance record concerning the electronics equipment speaks for the job that these two men accomplished.

The squadron got a set of new B-29s from Martin, Omaha, and each crew was assigned its own aircraft. Training missions were flown almost daily, and every man was scored, from the airplane commander to the lowest-ranking mechanic on the flight line. The 320th Troop Carrier Squadron was activated, and it began to provide logistical support immediately, initially under the command of Chuck Sweeney and later under the command of John Casey.

In January, the ground echelon was shipped out. They proceeded by surface vessel from Seattle, Washington, to Tinian, Mariana Islands. Various other ground elements of the 509th went into effect during this period, and all of them underwent intensive training, both as individual elements and as functioning components of the group. Col. Tibbets and his staff oversaw the entire operation, but time was running out.

On Wednesday, June 20, 1945, all fifteen of the men shipping out that day reported to the flight line. Beser soon discovered that Lt. Arthur D. Henderson and his crew from the 320th Troop Carrier Squadron had drawn the duty of transporting them all from Wendover to Tinian. As they left the States, no one had a clue when the gimmick would be ready or what the plans were for when it was.

One of the wonders of World War II was the speed with which air power matured. At the outset of World War II, twin-engine transports had hardly come into their own domestically. From the start of the war in 1939 until June

1945, a period of slightly less than six years, four-engine aircrafts were built, tested, and placed into service, forming a logistical support for the two-ocean wars and changing transoceanic flying from a stunt to an everyday occurrence. The speeds at which these services developed and mobilized and the efficiency of the organizations involved were hard to fathom.

The men left Wendover Air Force Base early that morning and landed twenty-five hours later at Hickam Field, Hawaii, where the scars of the Pearl Harbor attack still lingered.

The unit stayed at Hickam for ten hours and was assigned temporary quarters in the main barracks, where the men would get in another eight-hour sleep and the airplane would get another inspection. Their takeoff was scheduled for 1700 local time.

After about four hours, part of which Beser spent inspecting the damage inflicted on the building by the Japanese and eating in the mess hall where so many had died, he contacted some local electronics specialists, who took him into Honolulu for some sightseeing. This was strictly against protocol but evidently a common occurrence.

The next morning, the crew continued on to the Marianas. They left Hickam on time and headed for Johnston Island, a little spot in the ocean developed by Pan American World Airways to support their early Pacific operations. They arrived on according to the flight plan and refueled the airplane and their stomachs in this artificial paradise. The menu consisted of hamburgers, cheeseburgers, Coke, and milk. The layover on Johnston Island lasted about one hour. From there, they continued west to the island of Kwajalein. The 393rd approached their destination at around 0200 hours.

Suddenly, it was like the Fourth of July. Antiaircraft fire erupted all around them. Art kinked the airplane, and there was one more salvo, this time behind them. Art explained to Beser, "We just flew over the island of Wotje. It's still occupied by the Japs." They had been briefed to fly a dogleg around this island, but for some reason, the warning had been overlooked. Shortly after this episode, they landed safely on Kwajalein.

This landing was the next-to-last stop on the journey from Hawaii to Tinian. They left within the hour and sailed west into the dawn of June 23. At about 1000 local time, they landed on Tinian, nineteen hours and fifteen minutes after leaving Honolulu. The entire trip had taken almost three days, with thirty-four hours and five minutes spent in the cabin and cockpit of a four-engine, C-54 transport. Beser could not help but marvel at the equipment and system that made this trip routine.

Those already on Tinian, including some of Beser's colleagues from his old outfit, had anticipated the 393rd's arrival. The 504th greeted them when their airplane rolled to a stop on its hardstand in the 393rd revetment area. Bill Stallings had with him Chief Warrant

Officer Karl Pendray. Beser hadn't seen either one of them since he left Fairmont, Nebraska, over a year earlier. Those in the 504th had no clue what the 393rd had been up to. They were bubbling over with news about the various fellows in the old group when Stallings, or Shorty, as they had called him, let his curiosity get the better of him.

"What are you guys up to?" he asked. "The whole immediate world in the 313th would give their eyes and teeth to get their hands on one of your airplanes." He drooled over the B-29s. "They have the newest engines, water injection for more power at takeoff, Curtis electric-paddle blade propellers, air-actuated bomb-bay doors, and all of the turrets, except those in the tail, which have been removed. What *are* you doing with them?"

Beser replied, "Shorty, even if I knew, I couldn't tell you."

By then, Beser had learned how to pick up information without giving much away. Regardless of the secrets, he was happy to be reunited with some of his old fellows he had met at either Boca Raton or in Orlando. They taught him more about the Japanese tactics than he could have ever learned on his own. By then, it had already been decided he would fly with the "gimmick," but the combat virgin did not yet know how he would prepare.

Lt. Beser began discussing his plans with Dr. Edward Doll, who had been his primary technical contact with the project people at Wendover. Beser had devised a plan whereby he would fly with one or more of the crews on any practice missions. This was to be done for three reasons. First, Beser wanted people to get used the idea that if he were assigned to their crew for a mission, he would be adding several antennas to their aircraft and about three hundred pounds of equipment. Second, he wanted as much exposure to the Japanese electronic environment as he could get as rapidly as he could get it. Finally, he wanted to assure himself that the procedure that he planned to employ was well thought-out and tested.

Beser discussed his plans briefly with Col. Tibbets and more fully with Col. Tom Classen, his deputy. Maj. James Hopkins was the Squadron Operations Officer, who Beser had known since his Orlando days. It was his job to order him to carry out his plans.

According to one of Beser's lifelong friend, he told a story, "Beser punched out Gen. LeMay. LeMay said to his face, 'Had I know you were a kike, I never would have let you fly the missions." His friend insisted Jake never really elaborated on what "punched out" meant, but he doubted Beser physically assaulted the general.

"The 509th *was* a 'cowboy' outfit," revealed Beser's friend. "They got away with 'non-army-standard' protocol. It is true the men worked hard for Col. Tibbets, who made them practice until they got it right every time. As old Jake said, 'Perfection comes with great difficulty and is seldom achieved.'"

The men of the 509th composite group became the envy of the other outfits stationed on Tinian. An anonymous writer once facetiously wrote,

Into the air the secret rose,
Where they're going, nobody knows.
Tomorrow they'll return again,
But we'll never know where they've been.
Don't ask us about results or such
Unless you want to get in Dutch.
But take it from one who is sure of the score,
The 509th is winning the war.

*　*　*

As the war in Europe wound down, the war in the Pacific Theater heated up, along with the unbearable summer. In April, President Roosevelt passed away, and Harry Truman moved into the White House as the new president. Up until that time, the assumed president had never heard of the Manhattan District. Secretary Stimson, the secretary of war at the time, pulled him aside and said, "Hey, Harry, there's something you ought to know," followed by words to the effect of, "You've got a superweapon on your hands, and you're going to have to decide whether or not we use it."

Commander In Chief, Harry Truman said at his desk, "The buck stops here." He had people studying problems and doing the groundwork to form the basis of his decisions, but all paths converged on the Oval Office. Truman had more advisers and more advice than he ever knew existed, but *he* called the shots, and he knew it.

On July 16, 1945, the United States conducted a test, codename Trinity, at 5:00 a.m. in the New Mexican desert just north of Alamogordo. It wouldn't be a historic American event, though, if it wasn't surrounded by lore and rumor. They say a blind man in San Francisco saw light when this thing went off. They say the United States delayed the Potsdam meeting to coincide with the planned Trinity test of the first live atomic bomb in Alamogordo. No sufficient documentation ever turned up to support that as a significant claim.

All kinds of stories have come out about it, but the truth of the matter is, the one piece of data that the crews of the strike planes really needed out of that test, they never got. The weather was bad the morning of the Trinity test. They dispatched what they thought was one of their more reliable crews from Wendover to take about the same position over the test site as the dropping aircraft would take over the target in Japan. The pilot never made it. He was about twenty miles away from the target when the Trinity test went off. The young crew of the *Enola Gay* would have to carry out the mission prepared to die.

When Truman got word at Potsdam that the test was successful, he made a casual "oh, yeah" joke on the way out of the conference room. He leaned over to Stalin and said,

"By the way, we have this new superbomb. It's atomic." Stalin didn't bat an eyelid. He didn't have to; he already knew about it. He knew how it worked. He knew the whole story. He had an Austrian refugee embedded in the British team working at Los Alamos: Klaus Fuchs, who was feeding the data out of there as fast as he could get his hands on it. Despite their best efforts to keep the place airtight, they couldn't always do it.

On the morning of Monday, July 16, the answer to the question *When will the gimmick be ready?* was made apparent to the men of the 393rd. They arranged ten airplanes to send to the Empire. This meant that all the service activities, including Beser's, were working full steam. Beser's sergeants knew their jobs well and needed very little help from Lt. Homa or himself. Someone had to be around in the event that any schedule conflicts arose with the other sections or if any unusual paperwork had to be signed. Beser felt like a fifth wheel. Homa and the sergeants did it all. Beser spent more time in operations and in the tech area than he did on the flight line. The fellows assured him not to worry about it, and he didn't. They kept him informed on a timely basis so that he would not be embarrassed if his superiors asked him a question. *The fact that we never had one piece of our equipment malfunction while we were out there is a tribute to the job that these men performed,* Beser later wrote.

Ten airplanes were going to be dropping full-scale Fat Man replicas- called pumpkins for the oblong size. The pumpkins carried no electronics and were filled with ten thousand pounds of Torpex, a fairly new high explosive developed by DuPont. This was about the equivalent of the British Grand Slam, the most destructive weapon dropped in Europe.

The name of this game was to initiate the Japanese to the idea that from now on, they would be seeing single B-29s over their empire that might be doing something other than taking reconnaissance photographs. This would add further strain to their already taxed defenses. In a few days, the 393rd would further modify these tactics to simulate those who they would ultimately use when their new weapons arrived.

Beser's crew was briefed to go to the city of Toyama, located at the center of the northern coast of Honshu at the southern end of Toyama Bay off the Sea of Japan. It was an industrial city and a fishing port. Their assigned target was a fish-oil processing plant located right alongside an inlet from the bay and very near a suspension bridge. Although the city had been bombed several times, this plant had somehow escaped. The output of this plant was vital to the manufacture and maintenance of aircraft and ship instruments, giving it high priority as a bombing target.

They made landfall at Hamamatsu and from there flew direct to Toyama. This put them over the main island of Honshu for almost two hours. They were flying at thirty-two thousand feet, simulating the tactics that they would use in a few weeks with the real weapon. From this altitude,

Beser's radio horizon was over two hundred miles in every direction. This was the radar officer's first comprehensive look at Japan's electronic environment. This kept him quite busy and allowed him to take many radio samples home on his wire recorder; tape hadn't been invented yet.

He viewed it as an excellent introduction as his view took in Osaka and Nagoya on his left and Yokohama and Tokyo on his right. The samples that he brought home on wire allowed analysis to be done under less strenuous circumstances. He reported to his project people that on this trip, he had found nothing to cause any concern.

The bombardier Mike Angelich did his usual good job of placing the bomb on the target. The strike photographs showed that not only was the plant hit, but the blast from the Fat Man Pumpkin had also twisted the suspension bridge. In one picture, a bus was still in midair and falling from the bridge into the inlet down below.

The entire mission took thirteen hours. The crew encountered no opposition and only light anti-aircraft fire in the target area. Upon return, they were served several ounces of good whiskey and were interrogated by the intelligence staff. This trip also earned Beser his first combat-mission credit.

Four days later, on July 24, Beser went again, this time to the city of Nihama on the island of Shikoku. It continued like this for a while. July 26, Yaizu. July 29, Ube.

A few days prior, people who Beser hadn't seen for a while—and some he had never seen—began showing up on the island. They continued to come through the end of July. They brought with them tales of a highly successful test that was conducted in the New Mexico desert near Alamogordo. Capt. Parsons was rumored to have brought pictures of the test with him. RAF Wing Commander Leonard Cheshire arrived, and Beser was told that he would be representing the United Kingdom and Prime Minister Clement Atlee. Beser easily surmised something big was in the wind. Men that Beser knew as civilians at Wendover appeared on Tinian as GIs. The tech area was crawling with people. At about the time Beser returned from Ube, Col. Tibbets grounded him until further notice. Beser wrote that Tibbets told him, "Keep it to yourself, but we will probably be going in a few days."

Beser didn't have to say anything. Almost on their own, the rumors began to fly.

* * *

19

HATSUNO AND SHIZUO NAKAMOTO, TWENTY-ONE AND TWENTY-FOUR YEARS OLD

A single ant is weak, but a colony is unstoppable. The Asian Network of Trust-Hiroshima (ANT-Hiroshima) uses this philosophy to foster a peaceful world. One person can desire peace, but a colony creates it. ANT-Hiroshima is a network built on peace initiatives, from building schools in Pakistan to spreading the seeds of trees that survived the atomic bombs. When I met Tomoko Watanabe, ANT's founder, she almost instantly folded me into her trust. Tomoko-san, as she insisted I call her, felt more like my mother than a coordinator. "You know, Ari means 'ant' in Japanese," she taught me. "I have ANT-Hiroshima, and you're the Hiroshima Ant."

That is the remarkable thing about Hiroshima. It's a place where peace isn't just an idea; it is a practice. I have been on a mission to meet survivors, and in the spring of 2013, Tomoko Watanabe and Keiko Ogura were on a mission to help me succeed. Ogura-san translated most of my interviews in Hiroshima, and Tomoko-san organized all of the meetings. Beyond that, she made sure I had dinner every night, rides if I needed them, and a roof over my head in a comfortable home. She didn't do it out of obligation or with any ulterior motive. She did it with love and devotion to a peaceful world. She would do it for anyone. She takes any chance she has to bring together two people from opposite sides of any conflict, past or present. She believes peace is like a muscle that must be exercised.

One night, she had arranged a special party. The guests of honor were a couple I had thought I would never see again. She worked in collaboration with the Sadako Legacy, who in 2012 had introduced me to them—the ninety-one-year-old Hatsuno Nakamoto, once employed at a rest house at the site of what is now called the Atomic Bomb Dome, and her husband, a former engineer on the famous Yamato warship.

Reports vary about what Hatsuno-san remembers, but according to her, a few days before the bomb dropped, the US Air Force dropped hundreds of leaflets. Written in Japanese with a picture of President Truman, they said something to the effect of, "Hiroshima is going to be destroyed in order to free the people from imperialism." It warned citizens to escape to the countryside.

Authorities threw the leaflets away immediately and ordered ordinary people to do the same.

I used to work next to the Hiroshima Prefectural Industrial Promotion Hall. It was a center for celebrations and cultural expos. One time, the beautiful, dome-shaped hall hosted the National Confections Expo, featuring candy from all over the country. It was one of my favorite places in Hiroshima.

I was supposed to be there that morning, but an air-raid warning made me thirty minutes late. I was in Hiroshima Station, waiting for a train and chatting with a friend on the platform. I saw, flying high up in the sky, a B-29 about the size of my fist. It dropped something and turned sharply to fly away. I followed its tail as it escaped. I didn't know where it was going. I simply thought it was beautiful. I remembered the plane and the warnings from the day before. Others had noticed the B-29, too, and I heard people murmur to one other, "Did it drop more propaganda?"

At that instant, I felt it on my skin, like a hot pressure, and then an explosion blew me off the platform. I woke up at the bottom of a trench, which might have been a train line. I didn't know how I had gotten there or how far away I had been thrown, but an old woman was trapped with me. We both panicked, and the woman screamed and rubbed her wounded arms. I saw a way out and pushed through to the street. Before I had time to wonder where everyone had gone, including the woman I was just with, I heard "Help me!" slowly rise out of the debris, and ghostly-looking people started to creep out of destroyed houses. I recognized one woman as someone I worked with.

"Wow, we're alive!" I said, running up to her. "We're still here, and we have each other, but we shouldn't be here!"

One of my shoes had been blown away. I thought maybe it wasn't practical to wear only one shoe, so I tossed away the other one, and we tried to run to my friend's house. It was hot like any summer day. The surface of the road seared my feet. I regretted giving up that other shoe. I shouldn't have thrown it away, but at the same time, I was glad I was alive.

We ran five kilometers to Kaitaichi, near Hiroshima. When we arrived, I passed out. The neighborhood my friend lived in was called Sakacho, and her neighbor took note of the injured people who were coming back from Hiroshima. He contacted my parents, and they came to pick me up. My body felt like it was sinking deep into the sea; I could no longer stand up. My parents had to carry me home, allowing me to rest as much as I needed along the way. We had no medicine. I tried to wash my burns in the seawater. I was happy to be alive. I didn't want to die, but it wasn't my choice. It was up to fate. So many around me died, even ones who weren't burned. To this day, I feel like my life was given to me.

*   *   *

Mr. Nakamoto had remained silent through his wife's testimony and felt the need to speak up about his own experience, though he was far from the city center.

I was in Kure. I used to work in construction on battle ships. On August 6, we could see the mushroom cloud rising from the center of Hiroshima City, but it was impossible to reach it.

By the next day, my father's neighbor hadn't returned to the house, so my father went into Hiroshima to look for him. He was gone all day, wandering around the whole city.

Father came back with two onigiri, or rice balls. At the time, we couldn't get white rice, so getting two was a treat. He had eaten half of one and saved the rest for us. When he returned home in the evening, he told my mother, "I had onigiri; they are delicious."

But my mother said, "It might be polluted or dirty; children shouldn't eat that." Mother threw the rice balls away. So my brother and sister and I didn't eat any, but my father had, and it turned out that they *were* affected by radiation.

When he digested the onigiri, he felt his internal organs melting from the inside. His gums and rectum bled. There were no doctors, and there was no remedy. We couldn't tell what kind of sick he was, and we had no information about radiation or the symptoms.

By September, he had died.

My neighbors and a lot of people searched for their families in the city; they were also affected by the bomb's radiation. They lost their hair, had internal problems, and died.

I don't know what to say about the imperialism and militarism we believed in. I was involved in the construction of the battleship called *Yamato*. I tested, operated, and finished it by December 8, when the Pacific War started. Clearly at the time, I felt we had made this amazing battleship, and we would be OK. *We are going to win*, I remember thinking. I feel embarrassed to have subscribed to that.

People burned by the atomic bomb tried hiding their scars. It is something we didn't always want the public to know. Even I didn't know my wife was a survivor until after we were arranged. Only recently have we had more opportunities to tell our stories. All I can do is talk and hope that people listen.

*   *   *

20

SAND IN THE WATER

1945

Everyone based on Tinian that wasn't part of the 509th thought they were merely a bunch of bad boys who didn't have enough combat experience. Beser and his men had only accomplished a total of thirteen solo flights over the mainland, and no one else knew what they were up to. The 393rd Bomb Squadron members were considered the jokers of the island. The rest of the bomb squadrons groups stationed on Tinian had been over the mainland twenty times over. They all thought they could do a better job, whatever the job was. Gen. Arnold had made a decision that the 393rd Bomb Squadron and Paul Tibbets were going to drop the gimmick, and that's the way it was. They were briefed to prepare for any time after August 1, when the weapon would be ready.

The essential components for the first bomb were sent out on the cruiser *Indianapolis*. A Japanese submarine had trailed the battle cruiser. The Japanese submarine was unaware of what the *Indianapolis* was carrying, as it would have alerted the mainland if it had known. After delivering its atomic payload at Tinian in the Marianas Islands twelve miles north of Guam, the nuclear transporter was sunk, at the cost of a tremendous loss of life. For the superstitious airmen, it was a bad start to the mission.

The men of the 509th were given their general briefing on August 1. The only thing holding them back was the weather over Japan. The men on Tinian had a weather guru out there with them. He was a walking weather statistician for the air over the Pacific area. He had made a lifelong study of meteorology and had been tracking it over his entire career. He had a very heavy document that he carried with him, and he must have had records from every year since they opened the doors to Japan in 1860-something. He told them that the weather would be clearing and that they would be able to go the night before the sixth.

The strike mission general briefing, a closed meeting, began at midnight. Col. Tibbets gave the pep talk and flag-waving portion. He thanked everyone for their help and cooperation. "Tomorrow," he said, "the world will know that the 509th composite helped end the war."

Gen. Parsons took the dais. "We brought a movie of the weapon test in New Mexico to give you some idea of what to expect." He tried to play it for the anxious crowd, but it didn't work. As can happen, the movie projector malfunctioned. As a substitute for the film, Parsons gave a tutorial lecture and chalk talk. "The gimmick has the equivalent yield of twenty thousand tons of TNT."

As one of the few people privy to such knowledge, Beser had anticipated this being the case, but he still couldn't equate the one-pound blocks of TNT used in training to twenty thousand tons. Parsons drew a picture of the mushroom cloud and described the flash of light that would accompany it.

Finally, Chaplain Bill Downey delivered his prayer. "We ask you, oh Lord, for your protection and divine guidance for these young men who are to fly tonight."

The briefing concluded at 0030, and they relocated to the mess hall. The miracle worker, Capt. Charlie Perry, produced pineapple fritters in response to a special request. Beser stuffed up on oatmeal, eggs, and a mutton chop. A quart of milk and several slices of GI bread with butter sufficed for dessert. He ate what he thought could be his last meal. *If anything happens, I'm going out on a full stomach.*

The crew arrived at the flight line at about 0200, just in time to see the weather observers taxi out for takeoff. The hardstand where the airplane stood gave all the appearances of a Hollywood film premiere. There were klieg lights and movie cameras in abundance. Still photographers popped their flashbulbs. This was all being done by the military, except for the work of Bill Laurence of the *New York Times*, who represented the civilian press. The airplane now had a name. Col. Tibbets had his mother's name, Enola Gay, painted on the nose in plain block letters. Even though

Bob Lewis was the commander of the plane, it was pretty much assumed that the colonel would take this one.

Just prior to boarding the *Enola Gay* for takeoff, Ed Doll handed Beser a small piece of paper no bigger than an old-fashioned special-delivery stamp with four radio frequencies written on it. These were the frequencies that the proximity devices in the weapon operated on. Doll told him, "Eat it before you bail out."

Because the device would be detonating via radar, it was Beser's job to scramble their frequency so no one could figure it out. If the frequency were discovered, the enemy could detonate the bomb in midair or even before it dropped. If they were not detected, Beser would consider himself a glorified babysitter.

At around 0300, they loaded into the airplane to take off. Sergeant Lathrop thought he was doing Beser a favor by tossing his parachute pack up into the airplane for him. Beser noticed in horror that he had tossed it by holding the D-ring at the end of the rip cord. The chute should have popped open right then and there, but it hadn't. Upon further inspection, it seemed that while it had been on the Jeep waiting to be put aboard, someone had either sat on it or stepped on it and bent the pins that held it closed. Beser would have been in tough shape had he needed to use it. The fellows quickly found him another pack.

The takeoff roll was a typical Tibbets maneuver. He was used to his heavy airplane. Despite being nicknamed Little Boy, the bomb weighed nearly ten thousand pounds.

With the brakes locked, Tibbets brought the engines up to full power. As they began to roll, he held the nosewheel down until the last possible moment and then gently rolled the trim tab. The airplane leaped into the air. For the next several miles, he held the airplane level. As the airspeed built up, he started a slow, steady climb to his cruising altitude. Beser went forward as soon as possible for one last word with Parsons and Morris Jeppson, the assistant weaponier, and then returned to the aft compartment. He had not slept in twenty-seven hours, so he sprawled out on the floor and fell into a deep slumber.

About five and a half hours after takeoff, *Enola Gay* approached the island of Iwo Jima. They rendezvoused with the other two airplanes that would accompany the delivery of Little Boy. They received weather reports from the three flights that had left Tinian one hour ahead. Based on these weather reports, they decided on their target.

As they neared the island, the crew decided Beser had slumbered long enough. They further decided that his alarm should be a hit in the head from a piece of fruit rolled down the tunnel connecting the two major compartments of the plane. A wager was made, and the men up front took turns rolling oranges down the tunnel. The one who woke him collected the pot. Beser never found out who won, but regardless, it was time for him to shake the cobwebs out of his hair and get ready for his job.

Right on schedule, at about 0900 Tinian time, the weather reports began coming in. Buck Eatherly and his crew over Hiroshima reported one-tenth coverage, meaning it was essentially wide open. Ralph Taylor and John Wilson had gone to Kokura and Nagasaki. Their reports were equally good. Because Hiroshima had been briefed as a primary target, the *Enola Gay* crew determined to go there.

There are several legends about this decision. Beser wasn't on the flight deck, so he couldn't say for sure who made the final decision. But he did know there was little discussion about it, and Paul Tibbets transmitted it to the rest of the crew.

From Iwo Jima, the *Enola Gay* and company headed straight for Hiroshima. Their track took them over the western part of Shikoku, west of Kure, and straight into the target city. As they neared Japan, Beser began to detect the familiar Japanese early-warning radar. Soon, it was locked on to them. He did his job and scrambled the frequency. As the distance to Hiroshima closed, he made an intensive scan over the radio signals in the part of the airway spectrum where the crew's proximity devices would operate. He found the area "as clean as a hound's tooth."

He could hear Parsons and Jeppson on the intercom. They made one final check of the weapon. A little earlier, Jeppson's alert box had momentarily lit up like a Christmas tree, and it seemed as if they had a sick weapon on their hands, but in less than a minute, the problem had been fixed.

Just before 0815, Beser overheard the navigator telling the bombardier, "We're over our initial point," the landmark from which they were to formally begin the bombing run. With that call, they opened the bomb-bay doors and actuated a radio tone signal. This signal alerted the *Enola Gay*'s escorts that they were about to bomb. They now got ready to do their jobs: release instruments and take photographs.

They said, "Bombs away!" and the airplane was put into a rather violent escape maneuver: a sharp right turn whereby the vehicle loses about three thousand feet in order to build up airspeed and turn 158 degrees in about two minutes. It was supposed to put fifteen miles between the explosion and the airplane. The bomber continued moving forward and turning to the side. Jake was pinned to the floor during that escape maneuver. At precisely 08:15:15 Hiroshima time, the tone signal stopped, the bomb was released, and a new era in man's inhumanity began. "I never saw the intact city of Hiroshima," wrote Beser, "but I saw a flash."

The crew had been issued welders' goggles, but Beser couldn't wear his because he couldn't see well enough through them to do his job. He was buried in the back of the airplane, which had a deep-green liner and tiny windows. Any light that came in would just be absorbed, so he wasn't really concerned. The guys at the window had to be apprehensive, though, because they were right in the light's path. The flash erupted outside, and the next thing Beser heard in his headset was the voice of the copilot saying, "My God, look at that son of a bitch blow!"

Beser had brought along a special disk recorder to make a record of the crew's reaction at the time of the explosion. He walked around documenting the historic moment. Col. Tibbets informed the crew, "We have dropped and witnessed the world's first atomic bomb." When queried, he reminded them, "Lt. Beser will be recording us for posterity, so keep it clean."

Everyone made a statement for the record; none was very profound. They had never seen anything like it. Once they finished the escape maneuver, Beser grabbed a window seat. The mushroom cloud had already passed their flight level of thirty-two thousand feet, but it continued to be quite active. It rapidly changed color from red to purple before it finally stayed a dark gray.

On the periphery of this boiling mess, fires broke out. It was obvious that enormous damage had been inflicted on the city and its inhabitants. It would have taken a host of airplanes to do what they had just done. The bizarre nature of the scene below captured everyone's attention. It was like going down to the shoreline and kicking into the tide and then watching the sand billow in the water. That's what the atomic bombing of Hiroshima looked like to Jacob Beser—like sand in the water.

*   *   *

21

TSUTOMU YAMAGUCHI, TWENTY-NINE YEARS OLD, PART 1

In the hills of Nagasaki, tucked in the nook of a valley and forest broken apart only by houses, lives Toshiko Yamazaki, the daughter of Tsutomu Yamaguchi. A short woman with shoulder-length silver curls; wide, thick-rimmed glasses; and a silver track jacket, she stood invitingly with her daughter and her grandson at the entrance of her home when we arrived. Our group comprised two filmmakers; our translator, Tomoko Maekawa; and me. We sat down in the same family room I had seen the night before in the documentary about her father, which I had watched to prepare myself. The director, Mr. Inazuka, gave the OK for us to start talking while he filmed his next documentary. She swallowed, looked at the camera and then at me, and said, "When your grandfather came here in 1985, he made a lot of hibakusha angry."

I suddenly felt as though this could be a trap, a ploy to attack me on camera, as if doing so somehow mattered. "He said he felt no guilt for what he did. I could have brought you here to yell at you for your family, but I'm not going to do that. My father taught me to be above apologies. Just seeing each other, and meeting together, is the honor. I don't like to think about apology. Meeting together is very important. This is what we can do to have a good relationship."

Until I turned twelve, about fifteen years after the bombing, my father was bandaged. His injuries on his arms never cured completely for fifteen years. From seeing that, I came to understand atomic bombs were different from other bombs.

Still, the effects of radiation didn't stop. When my father was eighty, in the summertime, his arm turned black. It wasn't sunburn. It must have been because of radiation. Whenever he got a cold, he almost always got pneumonia.

I got a cold when I was eleven years old and in about fifth grade in school. I started bleeding from my nose. My mother was surprised. I was the second generation of two Hibakusha. Doctors discovered that I had a very low white blood cell count. I was hospitalized quite a long time. I hated the hospital.

After three months in the hospital with no special treatment working, I asked if I could leave. Soon after that, I got sicker and returned to the hospital.

I left the hospital without the doctor's permission. When I was lying on in my bed, I felt like I could sink deep into the mattress. The doctors had no idea what was wrong, but they had to call it something, so they called it children's rheumatism. Another friend of mine, also a second-generation Hibakusha, had the same problem and the same symptoms as me.

*   *   *

My grandparents' generation worshipped photos of their emperor and his family, but my father was not fond of the practice. When an air raid occurred, loyal citizens grabbed the photo of their emperor before their own belongings. He could not understand why we would worship a man based on his family rank.

My mother was raised by her aunt and uncle. By that time, most young people had been sent to the battlefield. Almost no engineers were designing, and they were in demand. My father didn't go to war because he was needed at home to scheme up battleships. In 1934, when he was eighteen, like many young men his age, he was hired by Mitsubishi Heavy Industries. By the time the war broke out, he had achieved the rank of nautical designer.

Even though my father never talked about whether he wanted to go to the front lines or not, I don't think he wanted to. He knew that Japan could not win. From his working situation, he knew Japan had a lack of everything. His uncle had gone to America and come back and told him how strong and how big it was. "There's no way Japan could win a war against America," his uncle would say.

Father and Mother's newborn son, born in 1943, died from a bad cold due to a lack of medicine. Two years later, they had a second baby, my brother, who was three months old when father had to leave for Hiroshima. The Japanese military wanted more ships as an effort to boost its defenses against an impending invasion. Father had been working as an engineer and ship designer for Mitsubishi Heavy Industries, and he was transferred to Hiroshima to help design new battle machines. The requisitioned workers were ordered to make as many ships as possible.

On the train ride to Hiroshima, Father and his colleagues, Sato and Iwanaka, saw that all of the cities had been destroyed and burned out, bombed by the American forces. They thought that Hiroshima would be the same.

"We better not go. There won't be any use for us. It will probably be destroyed," one of them said. Contrary to their expectations, Hiroshima was a glimmering oasis of life in a vast desert of destruction.

Every day for the next three months, the three men from Nagasaki routinely went to the factory, but gradually, Father started to feel uneasy. It was quiet in Hiroshima: no bombs and no air-raid sirens. It was like the stalk of a cheetah before the big attack.

On the morning of August 6, the three Nagasakans were chatting about going home the next day. One said, "Should we buy our tickets today or just show up?"

"I doubt it will be busy," Father said. "We can just show up—" He suddenly realized he had forgotten his *inkan*, or name stamp. He needed it for work, so he ran back to his dormitory to retrieve it.

He was walking in a field near the factory. Everyone had gone to work, and it was the quiet moment of the day. Father was practically alone in a potato field, except for one woman carrying a white parasol, walking in the same direction as he was. The sound of a B-29 roared overhead, and the woman looked to the sky. He followed her gaze and saw two white parachutes coming down. Soon after the parachutes, he saw a giant flash and a wave of light.

The light, a white light the same color as exploded magnesium, was so bright it was as if the sun had fallen to the earth. Houses were blown away by the blast of wind coming toward Father. At nearly the same instant, he was whipped up in the blast and thrown into the irrigation ditches. After twisting several times in the air, he had landed on his right side, and his left side was totally burned.

He didn't know how long he had been knocked out, but when he regained his senses, he saw the mushroom cloud, and another on top of that one, growing blacker and blacker as it rose. The air was dark and dusty, and pieces of debris flew by. A sound like the noise of a film projector had brought him back to consciousness, but when he found the source of the sound, he couldn't believe what he was witnessing. It wasn't a projected image; it wasn't a movie. It was roof tiles falling from the mushroom cloud. Soon, the black rain started falling, too.

There was a river nearby. He limped over to a big tree to sit underneath it. He saw several children who were burned. At the time, the Japanese believed that burn victims should not drink water immediately. A new father himself, he had a natural instinct to help them, but he couldn't begin to think of how. He was severely burned, too, and needed to find a way to survive. The water from a nearby pipe was oily. He wouldn't drink it. He sensed it was dangerous, contaminated with something. When he saw the white light of the explosion, he thought it looked like poison. Maybe this was due to his technical experience, but he thought something was unnatural about it. The river was a little farther away from them, so he had to walk to it, but still, he wouldn't drink its water. He needed to find clean water.

Severely burned, he tried to reach the factory, but there was an air-raid shelter on the way. There, he met one female student laborer. She happened to have some palm oil—"from my parents, just in case," she said as she put it on Father's burns. The girl treated him and revealed just how severe his burns were. The shelter also contained a woman who was horribly burned, crying out in Korean.

On the way back to the dormitory, Father saw a group of children walking very quietly, like ghosts. Their skin was ripped off their bodies and hanging from their nails, and debris stuck out of their backs. Everybody, adult and child, was walking, but my father's eyes were drawn to the students.

He couldn't get back to the dormitory by any way he knew. All of the bridges had collapsed, and the river was full of dead bodies. People clung to them as if they were human rafts. The living were trying to make their way across. He went around the river. Along the banks, he saw many people who he thought were drinking water, but upon closer inspection, he realized they were dead in that position, having died after their last gulps of water.

The elementary-school children might have been at school together before the blast. They now made groups to walk home. Because of the heavy burns, though, it was difficult to distinguish the boys from the girls. It was hard to see anything besides charred flesh and dead skin hanging from their outstretched arms and dragging at their ankles. Some people were carrying their own internal organs, which hung from their bodies. It was a gruesome scene.

There was no dignity of humanity after the bomb. However, I have never heard my father express his pain. I think he was still wearing clothes then, but the burned part of his body had singed away, and soon the injured part swelled.

"Oh God, Kami-sama. Universe, forgive me. This is enough!" he cried.

When my father went back to the dormitory, he went to an industrial high school near the lodgings. Water was gushing from a broken pipe, and there he finally drank water.

He wanted to reach Koi so he could take a train back, like he had originally planned. The next day, the three men regrouped and set out to get back home. The train started at Koi Station across town. However, all of the bridges were blown out, and the roads were filled with debris and the dead and dying. They thought about crossing the river, but there were dead bodies floating in the current. My father's colleagues stopped him from crossing. He was totally burned, and they warned him not to enter; otherwise, his wounds would get infected from the bloody, murky water. Instead of crossing the river by walking, they chose to cross a nearby railway. They had to step across a wooden railway, taking care not to step between the boards and fall. Father was sick and dizzy, but he managed to cross the river.

When they finally got to the train station and were able to find seats, Father became very tired. He saw some water outside, but he didn't have enough energy to leave his seat.

The train station was full of people, and he couldn't move. Sato-san went back to the factory to tell them they were leaving, and my father and Iwanaka took the train toward Nagasaki. But Iwanaka got off the train in Kikitsu, before Nagasaki. My father arrived back at Nagasaki Station on the morning of the eighth.

*　*　*

22

MISSION'S A GO
1945

Wednesday, August 8, 1945, was a day of worries for everyone concerned with the mission for which they were due to depart at 0330 the next morning. The weather over Japan had deteriorated, and the forecast for the next twenty-four hours looked bleak. The test flight would go as soon as they had a clear window. After the test, the airplane would taxi to the special loading area to receive the weapon it would deliver that night. If any malfunctions developed during the test flight, a standby airplane had to be ready, so the ground crew remained on constant alert until the mission was underway.

The test drop happened just before noon, during a lull in the local flying. The men on the ground were startled to hear what sounded like a speeding freight train heading right for the field. This apparition suddenly ceased, only to be followed by a loud crump as the pumpkin bomb impacted the ocean several miles out. The positive results of the test were known immediately. Another major milestone had been passed. "Now we wait," said Beser to one of his officers.

General briefings were scheduled for the weather ships at 2230, and those in the strike element would be briefed at 0030. In both cases, the special briefings for the pilots, navigators, radar operators, bombardiers, and flight engineers would follow the general briefings.

Everyone was encouraged to get as much rest as possible, and the strike-element crews were told to sleep until midnight. At just about the time Beser thought he might be able to catch forty winks, Sergeant Edwin Bell, one of his mechanics, came to him and said, "This airplane needs one additional radar modification."

They were carrying auxiliary fuel tanks in the after-bomb bay. Beser requested that the power inverter for his equipment and the radar set be moved from the bomb bay to a compartment under the floorboards of the after-compartment. If an inverter went out at altitude or a fuse mounted on the inverter blew, they would be unable to do their jobs because they would have no satisfactory way to get into the bomb bay to make any repairs, short of depressurizing or coming down in altitude. In addition, Beser did not want to be playing with electrical equipment in the presence of gasoline vapors and an atomic bomb. Bell wanted him to bring some horsepower into the situation so that they could make this change.

Beser immediately contacted Capt. Cecil King, an engineering officer who, after casting a few aspersions as to his unsound state of mind, agreed that the work had to be done. Because it was only a ten-minute operation and the power cart was still running, they could do it immediately. Beser, a perfectionist, decided to go down to the flight line with them and determine for himself if anything else might have been overlooked.

When the strung-out radar man arrived at the flight line, he found that the inverter transfer had already been accomplished and the system tested. Everything seemed in order, so he returned to his living area and tried to get some rest. It was not to be, however. On the way back, Beser ran into Bill Laurence, who stopped him with an invitation to have a cold one at the club. He was going to fly this one with them, albeit with Fred Bock and his crew on one of the escort aircraft carrying scientific observers. Quite a few of the senior-project people were there, also. Beser joined this late-evening social until it was time to go to the briefing. He had not slept, but he did at least relax, listening to extremely educated people discussing things he barely understood.

Maj. Charles Sweeney and his team were named as the strike crew for this mission. Chuck was now the squadron commander, and as such, he had the option of selecting any of the squadron crews for this job. He chose Don Albury and Fred Olivi's crew, as he had most of his experience with them, and they had accompanied the *Enola Gay* to Hiroshima. This crew also had several of the pumpkin missions behind them. Paul had selected Chuck based solely on his experience in the B-29 test program. Although they all liked Chuck and had confidence in his ability as a B-29 pilot, there were those in the original cadre of the 393rd who felt that, based on combat experience and demonstrated valor, Tom Classen, their original squadron commander and now deputy group commander, would have been a more logical choice. Unfortunately, Maj. Classen was heading back to the States on a special mission for Col. Tibbets.

After the briefings ended, the crews for the next mission left en masse for the mess hall. The fare was as good, if not better, than the chow he had before leaving for Hiroshima, and once again Beser did justice to everything he had put on his tray. If anything went wrong this time, he was certainly not going to die on an empty stomach, although if the weather didn't cooperate, he might have one after all. There was still no reply from the Japanese, and thus no surrender. They received word: "Mission's a go."

*   *   *

23

TSUTOMU YAMAGUCHI, TWENTY-NINE YEARS OLD, PART 2

"Fifty years ago, America and the Soviets were caught up in the Cuban Missile Crisis, and the arms race was just beginning. In that generation, Hibakusha stood up under Senji Yamaguchi and started to work for peace against nuclear war, despite the American umbrella Japan was under. My father thought to stand up and talk about his experiences as a double survivor. My family stopped him. Mr. Senji Yamaguchi was greatly scarred, and so were the other Hibakusha. Even though inside my father was physically damaged, from the outside nobody could tell he was injured. 'It may show people that even after experiencing two bombs, you could survive and look healthy,' I told him. It's my fault he waited to speak," Toshiko revealed to me.

"My father had overcome and was beyond feelings of blame. He always said that both sides were wrong. It *was Japan that started the war, but using the atomic bomb was inhumane and shouldn't be accepted. Who did what shouldn't be discussed.*

"I think of both your grandfather and my father as victims of war, Ari-san. Probably your grandfather became ill and was also a hibakusha like my father." I nodded at the assertion. He had passed away from bone cancer as a result of plutonium exposure. "My father often lived by the philosophy of being beyond hatred. What we are doing is not at the level of apology. If we move past that, we should be able to achieve real peace," said Toshiko.

According to an Asahi Shimbun article published in 2013, "there were thirty-three confirmed double atomic bomb survivors as of 2001. In Hiroshima, the city's relief division does not know how many there are. In June 2011, after analyzing memoirs, the Hiroshima National Peace Memorial Hall for the Atomic Bomb Victims found that there may be three hundred seven such people."

As soon as father's train arrived in Nagasaki, he had his wounds tended to at the Shingozen elementary school, which was being used as a military hospital. After getting treatment, he looked for his wife. Out of fear of an air raid, my mother and my brother had moved since my father left, but he didn't know where they had gone. So he went back to his parents' house in Okeyamachi, in downtown Nagasaki. When they heard Hiroshima was destroyed, his parents did not think he had survived. Father was kneeling at our family shrine when his mother returned home. Surprised to see a figure in front of the altar, she asked, "Who is that? Do you have legs?" His mother, my grandmother, thought he was dead, and ghosts lack lower limbs.

When the news of his return spread, neighbors flocked to see him and ask what had happened to Hiroshima.

"A new, huge type of bomb was dropped," he revealed. "It's better to wear something white, because black can absorb heat, for one thing. Keep your windows open or duck as soon as the bomb goes off. The glass will turn into bullets."

That night, he had a high fever, but even though his condition was bad, on the next morning, August 9, he went in to work at Mitsubishi Heavy Industries. Because he was covered in bandages from head to foot, his colleagues could barely recognize him. The other workers were quiet when he told them what had happened.

"Hiroshima was destroyed with one bomb," he repeated, along with his advice. Unlike his neighbors, however, they didn't believe what he said.

"Tsutomu-san, you're a technician! You should know that what you're saying is not possible. How could one bomb destroy a whole city?"

"I was there. Look at my face; look at my bandages. I saw it."

They thought he had been driven insane. At that moment, he saw the same magnesium flash of light and instinctively ducked under the desk.

After he had hidden under the desk, he saw that towns were on fire outside. He thought it would be better to get out of the building, and without realizing how, he went up to the hill behind the back of the factory. His colleagues were either dead or severely burned. The section chief, who had been standing, was killed by flying glass shards.

In Hiroshima, he had witnessed the atomic bomb from the beginning, before it had exploded. He had seen the flash of light and the debris coming down from the mushroom cloud. He had seen everything. This time, he was inside and caught off guard. His experience in Hiroshima, for him, was greater than in Nagasaki. He always said that his experience in Hiroshima was much worse.

He noticed his bandages were gone, disappeared, his burned flesh now covered with dust. There was a watchtower on the hill, and he saw that the watchman had already died. The mushroom cloud billowed about a mile and a half away in the Urakami Valley, and he later expressed he had thought, *The mushroom clouds chased me to Nagasaki.*

*   *   *

24

MAYDAY! MAYDAY!

1945

As had happened on several previous nights, Dr. Ed Doll sought Beser out prior to takeoff and gave him a little slip of paper with the operating frequencies of the four proximity devices, once again with instructions to "eat it if you have to."

The assembly on the flight line this night in no way resembled the one that had gathered for the *Enola Gay*'s departure for Hiroshima. There was a decided absence of the Hollywood-premiere atmosphere, and most everyone was subdued. There was a sense that everyone just wanted to get it over with. Beser was beginning to feel the effects of his sleep deprivation, so he sat on the hood of the colonel's jeep until it was time to go. That time came and went, and they were still sitting there, waiting. Something was causing a delay in their departure.

Maj. Charles Sweeney, the pilot that night, went over to Capt. Tibbets several times. They removed themselves from the rest of the crew's presence and had several animated discussions. At one point, Fred Ashworth was made privy to the discussions, but neither Bill Laurence nor Beser could join in.

"It could be two things," said Beser to one of his enlisted men. "Either the weather over Japan is not clearing up as expected, or there's a problem with the bomb-bay fuel-transfer pump."

Sweeney and Capt. James Van Pelt came back to the jeep with their slide rules and a sheaf of papers. They evidently had worked out a new flight plan. At Tibbets and Ashworth's OK, the crew was given the signal to load up and go. Takeoff was routine and uneventful, and in less than three minutes after the wheels went up, Beser was on the floor, sound asleep.

The weather en route to Japan turned out to be worse than forecast, although it was expected to clear by the time they reached their target. Beser might have slept like a log on the way up to Hiroshima, but this night was far from easy. He and his radar team were in an unpressurized condition most of the way, and the air in the cabin was warm and soggy. After a while, they climbed to seventeen thousand feet, and things improved somewhat. Beser missed a display of Saint Elmo's fire, and the fellows later told him that it was "spectacular."

The dreary radar countermeasures officer was fully awake by 0912, when the *Great Artiste*, under the command of Capt. Freddie Bock, reached the Yakushima rendezvous point at bombing altitude. Maj. Jimmie Hopkins on the *Victor 90* had yet to arrive. After forty-five minutes, they could not wait any longer. In the meantime, the weather reports from Charles McKnight and George Marquardt had come through, and they were about the same for both Kokura and Nagasaki. Because Kokura had been briefed as a primary target, they set their course.

When they arrived at Kokura, it was obvious that visual bombing would be a problem. Yawata, the Pittsburgh of Japan, had been firebombed the night before and was still burning. Situated a few miles west of Kokura, it was sending smoke and haze over their target, compounding the problem for the bombardier, Kermit Behan. After approximately two-thirds of a run, Kermit said, "No drop." He could not get a clear sight of his briefed aiming point.

Sweeney circled the area to try a second run. This time, they not only didn't drop, but they received antiaircraft fire. There was considerable conversation on the flight deck concerning remaining fuel and alternate flight plans. Chuck Sweeney and his flight engineer had a difference of opinion, but Fred Ashworth very clearly argued what he felt they should be doing and especially what they should not be doing. There was no time for a lengthy debate. They were burning fuel at the rate of four hundred gallons per hour.

"We should make one more pass at Kokura, and if we don't drop, then we should head for Nagasaki. If we are unable to get a visual at Nagasaki, then I, as Gen. Groves's deputy on this flight, will take the responsibility, and we'll make a radar run. From there, we can head down the coast of lower Kyushu and land in Okinawa," schemed Ashworth.

While that discussion was underway, Beser began to detect activity on the Japanese fighter control frequencies. In a few moments, it became obvious that they had scrambled some fighters, and before long, they would be looking for them.

Bock's car made its third pass at Kokura, and still no success. They headed across the Shimonoseki Straits and followed the coastline down and across to Nagasaki. As they left Kokura, after about one hour and several power cycles of turning on and off the weapon in the bomb bay, their tail gunner announced that he could see fighter aircraft breaking through the clouds below. As luck would have it, the Japanese fighters must have had a different target in mind because they abandoned pursuit.

Bock's car continued on to Nagasaki and found that the weather was no better there than it had been at Kokura; if anything, it was slightly worse. They were on a radar run to the city. Beser wrote in *his* memoir that Fred Ashworth, commensurate with his responsibility, paid close attention to the navigator's radarscope to be sure that it was Nagasaki they were approaching. He was monitoring the navigator-bombardier "talk-in" procedure they were following, whereby the navigator tracks the target on his scope and verbally gives the bombardier the data that he would have otherwise acquired visually with his bombsight.

Approximately twenty seconds before the bomb would have been released, a hole opened up in the clouds, and Behan saw what he thought was their briefed aiming point. "I've got it! I've got it!" he shouted.

The airplane lurched as the bomb was released, and Sweeney put it into a tight turn to the left to give them some distance from the explosion. After about forty-five seconds, Beser was again enveloped in the now-familiar warm white flash, and by the time he got to the window, a rapidly ascending mushroom cloud burned through what had been a Nagasaki suburb. There was time for only one circle of the area before they had to begin making tracks for Okinawa.

Only one thing disturbed Beser as they made their getaway: unlike in Hiroshima, this time, the plane had felt three shockwaves. Yet no one had seen any antiaircraft fire. They reasoned that the first shockwave was from the explosion itself; the second was a direct reflection under the airburst; and the third had to be from a wall of hills, informing them that they had hit the Urakami Valley and missed their target by at least a mile and a half.

They did not have enough fuel to go back and take another look. The flight engineer's latest calculation after they set up a reduced power glide from altitude was that it would be close, but they just might make it to Okinawa.

In the interim, the radio operator had alerted the air-sea rescue unit of their intentions.

Maj. Hopkins, who until then had not been seen nor heard from by Bock's car, put out a blind radio call. "Chuck, where the hell are you?"

This startled the entire crew, but once the bomb had been dropped, the need for radio silence no longer existed. Sweeney responded to Hopkins, saying, "We're en route to Yontan Airstrip on Okinawa. If there is any way, try to catch up with us there."

When he realized that he had missed his rendezvous, Hopkins decided to loiter somewhere between Kokura and Nagasaki in the hopes of finding them. When he was about to abandon his wait and go to Okinawa to refuel, he saw the mushroom cloud rise above Nagasaki and decided to give them a call. As they neared Okinawa, the radio traffic was horrendous. There was a raid of Liberator bombers returning from Japan, along with their fighter escorts. Sweeney broadcast a Mayday distress signal, which theoretically should have cleared the air, but it didn't. "Mayday. Mayday…Mayday. Mayday…"

*   *   *

25

SAKUE SHIMOHIRA, TEN YEARS OLD

Takahashi Nagai had leukemia and was given three months to live. That was before he was exposed to the plutonium bomb accidentally dropped over the Urakami Valley about a mile away from Nagasaki City Center. He ended up living for a decade longer than he was predicted. A Catholic convert, he became known as the saint of Urakami. When he fell ill again, the Society of Saint Vincent de Paul built a small hut for him outside of the shack he had made from the remains of his destroyed house. Nagai called it Nyokodo, or "As Thyself Hut," after Jesus's words "Love thy neighbor as thyself." At school, Dr. Nagai encouraged the young kids to write essays about the atomic bomb. He was especially impressed with the essay of a young girl who lived near him, Sakue Shimohira, one of the kids who used to steal the ripe silver berries off his tree in the spring.

Shimohira was picked to broadcast her essay on the radio. She said, "We don't have anything to eat, and we don't have anything to wear. I had a chance to meet Dr. Nagai from time to time, and he told us to love others as you love yourself, like from the Bible. Therefore, international friendship is very important, and he taught us to live on with courage." Sakue Shimohira said these things at such a young age, when she was only in junior high school. It was the first time she spoke publicly, but it would be far from her last.

Before the bombing, my family lived in Manchuria, one of Japan's colonies in China. I was three years old and my little sister was one year old when our father was killed. He used to work on the Japanese railway that was established in Manchuria. The Chinese people knew that the Japanese soldiers were brutalizing them, so in an act of revenge, they beheaded six Japanese, one of whom was my father. When I was five years old, my aunt and uncle rescued us from Manchuria and took us to live in Nagasaki. I was six years old when Pearl Harbor was attacked and the war started. I was a first-grader at the Shiroyama Primary School. When I was in second or third grade, our condition was not so bad, but by the end of third grade, we had serious shortages.

We were suffering from severe shortages of everything, including notebooks, shoes, and clothes. My brother was a teacher, but he was sent to train for a special attack corps, which would be known as the kamikaze.

My second brother wanted to become a military doctor, but he couldn't study in the darkness that power shortages provided him with every night. The direct family I had left was my mother and my little sister. We were taken care of by my uncle, whose family had two boys and one girl, but she was married. We all lived together three hundred meters from what would become the hypocenter of the atomic bomb Americans called Fat Man.

My brother died on the battlefield. My younger brother became a military student, and even I wished to become a doctor, but the conditions were not good for studying. We didn't have food, we walked barefoot to school, and we were trained to cover our eyes and ears with our hands and lie facedown during an air raid. That was our training. There was nothing to protect us but our spirit. "We can't want until we win" was a wartime motto.

We didn't have much to do for fun. We went to school every morning to study, but every time a warning was issued, we would be evacuated. We were always training for evacuation, always living like we would have to drop everything and run at any moment.

At primary school, we had about two thousand students, and five hundred were evacuated to the countryside. We always evacuated ourselves to the air-raid shelters, which were basically holes in the mountainside. And Nagasaki has no shortage of mountainside.

At night, electricity was not permitted because it would invite attack. We would have to stay in darkness. We dug a hole underneath the floor as an escape, so if a bomb were to fall in our neighborhood and destroy our house, we would have an escape route to an air-raid shelter on a nearby mountainside.

From time to time, air-raid alarms were issued, and we were actually bombed a few times, especially in the industrial area, which was largely run by Mitsubishi.

In those days, all the young people from fifteen to sixteen years old were working in place of the adults, who had gone to war. On the night of August 8, my brother, who was a military student, came home and told us that a new type of bomb had been dropped on Hiroshima. "Don't go out of the air-raid shelter even when the alarm is lifted." That was his warning.

Early in the morning of August 9, the air-raid warning siren started wailing. I was with my eight-year-old sister and my one-year-old nephew, whom I carried on my back. We three evacuated to the air-raid shelter. However, the warning was lifted, so I went out. I remembered my brother's warning that we should never go out of the shelter, so we went back in the hole. I was about eight hundred meters away from the hypocenter in the air-raid shelter.

I remember only a tremendous flash, not the blast. It blew me to the back of the hole, and people say there was a thunderous sound, but I don't remember it.

After some time, when I regained consciousness, someone tapped my shoulder. The hole was dark, but I could see the outlines of people who must have come inside when I was knocked out. Someone's eyeball hung from its socket, and some had their intestines spilled out on their lap. It was dark, but I could see all of their injuries.

I could see some vague light outside, which was how I could see in the shelter, but I couldn't find my sister or nephew. I called out my sister's name, and I heard her weak voice. She was underneath the corpses, and I pulled her out. My nephew had been blown into the back of the hole and crushed by a tatami mat, but he was alive. Nobody came to rescue us. The three of us were shivering in the hole. An old lady was moaning for water. Blood dripped from her shoulder, and a baby was on her back, but the baby was headless. She asked us for help, three helpless children. The next morning, I heard someone yell, "Hello! Is anyone there alive?" I could hear the voice, but I couldn't get out; there were so many dead bodies blocking the way.

That evening, someone came to rescue us, and at last I could get out of the hole. I could see nothing, nothing except for what remained of the Urakami Cathedral, a few primary schools with no windowpanes, and charred, black, dead bodies everywhere.

I looked for my house, but I couldn't find it. It was close to the riverside, and in the river, there were a lot of blackened bodies, some on the riverbed, some floating. They had gone there searching for water, but there was no fence on the banks, so they just dropped. They reached the steps and tried to drink. Then, they died one by one, and one by one, they floated. Finally, we found a body with un-burned hands that were my other sister's. I looked for my mother, but there were many dead, and I couldn't find her. A B-29 flew overhead, and we ran away to a nearby hole. But the hole was filled with people and we couldn't en-ter. That evening, my brother came to look for us. We had stayed awake for two days waiting for him to find us. When he finally did, we collapsed in his arms and fell asleep.

My little sister, my older brother, my nephew, and I were the only survivors. We continued to look for my mother, and I found a body that had nearly turned to ash. The ash had an artificial gold tooth, and we knew that it was hers.

The three of us were taken care of separately. Around the end of 1945, my aunt and uncle built a shack by col-lecting materials from the wasteland. We slept on the same place where our old house used to be. There was no elec-tricity, but at night, we could see the glowing bones left behind; a reaction from the phosphorous emitted by the bomb caused them to glow a greenish blue. We were three hundred meters from the hypocenter, and starting in 1946, we lived under American occupation. We suffered from lack of food, so we picked up some leftover scraps from American soldiers' garbage: bread, sausage, and whatever else remained.

We kept living under those conditions. Maggots appeared in my sister's wounds. We didn't have any money for medical bills, and she couldn't take it. She jumped in front of a train. Before doing so, she begged me to take my life along with her. In that situation, one can choose courage to live or courage to die. She chose the courage to die, and I chose the courage to live.

I almost ended my life, but when I stood in front of the train, a man I had met came to stop me. When I had found my mother burned to death, he had found his mother lying next to mine. He followed me to the train tracks that day, and when I was ready to jump, he stepped out and called to me to stop, saying, "Who can carry on the family name? Who can offer flowers to the victims? Don't do this. Live with me instead."

He convinced me, and I didn't jump.

*   *   *

26

THE FINAL CURTAIN
1945

In desperation, Sweeney told the navigator to fire everything they had. This had two results. First, from the amount of smoke pouring from every duct, the crew thought that a major fire had broken out in the back of the airplane. Two, some pilot in the traffic pattern sensed that the big bird was in trouble and peeled off. Those in the pattern behind him followed suit, and Sweeney was able to put her on the ground, although he came in high and fast, and when he touched down, it was indeed a controlled crash. As he came to the end of the runway, he was still rolling fast. His options were to go over the cliff or to make a ninety-degree turn. He opted for the latter, but he failed to warn those in the back that they were about to turn. The centrifugal force in the turn almost put them through the side of the fuselage. But they were on the ground, and no one was badly hurt.

As they trailed the "follow me" jeep to a hardstand where they could park the airplane, the two inboard engines drained their tanks and stopped. A mission couldn't get closer to disaster than the men who dropped the atomic bomb and nearly crash-landed getting back.

The people who met them were all excited. Several things had happened that morning. The Russians had invaded Manchuria, and Nagasaki had been A-bombed.

Beser wrote later, *You should have seen the expressions on their faces when we told them that we had just come from Nagasaki and had delivered the A-bomb there. In the crowd was a classmate of mine from Scott Field, Bill Ketel, whom I had not seen since the day we graduated two years earlier. Poor Bill, he had been assigned as a communications officer with a group of Liberators and had been island hopping behind McArthur ever since. He thought he was never going to get home. When he realized that we were not pulling his leg, and that we had indeed bombed Nagasaki just a little over two hours ago, he put his arm around my shoulder in a warm embrace as he struggled to hold back the tears. For him, the end of the war was now in sight, and he would be able to get back to civilization once more, an idea that was still quite remote a few hours ago.*

Fred Ashworth had given the radio operator a brief strike report right after the drop. In his memoir, he stated, *There was no contingency message covering all that had happened that morning, but since we were overdue, I felt that I owed them a statement to the fact that Nagasaki was the*

stricken target, there was a fuel problem, and we were head-
ing for Okinawa. My immediate concern at this point was to
get to Gen. Doolittle's headquarters and file a more complete
report.

Getting to Gen. Doolittle became a necessity when his communication officer paid no more attention to Ashworth than the tower had paid to the aircrew a little while earlier. Ashworth described the Wild West tactics he had to use to persuade the local bureaucracy that he was not only for real, but dead serious. Gen. Doolittle, after listening to his story, cleared the way for him to send his message back to Tinian.

When Fred Bock and his crew arrived on Okinawa, they confirmed that they had indeed hit the Urakami Valley and that the large Mitsubishi plant was the most likely target they had hit. To Gen. Doolittle, it seemed that this was a better choice than the city itself.

They waited for Jimmie Hopkins to arrive and refuel and then had to get out of there before the afternoon kamikaze raid came in. The operations clerk told them that if they looked down right after takeoff, they would be able to see the almost six hundred ships lying at the bottom of Buckner Bay, victims of the kamikaze. At the same time, there was a squad of marines who had been taken out of the lines just that morning, after thirty days of mopping up. They were a sorry, stinking sight; they had not yet had a chance to bathe and clean up. They clutched their rifles and souvenirs with equal fervor. Someone would have had one hell of a time trying to convince those kids that the war was already won.

All the way back to Tinian, about a five-hour flight, not much was said onboard the airplane. There was none of the euphoria that had been evident after the drop at Hiroshima. So far, they had experienced fourteen long and trying hours, and although it was now all downhill, it wasn't over yet. Each person onboard had pretty much the same ideas. Beser already knew that if there was to be another drop, he would go again. He thought over and over, *Japan, how soon before you spare your people more of this agony?*

They arrived back at Tinian late at night. There were no crowds to greet them, no medal-pinning ceremony; only those who would be involved with the interrogation were there. Admiral Purnell, in discussing their miss with Fred Ashworth, pointed out that this was perhaps a most fortunate happening, for if they had hit the city, the loss of life would have been far greater. He also described for them Gen. Farrell's concern when they were overdue. The poor old man had tossed his cookies. Now that was real concern, not feigned, and they all liked him and appreciated his feelings for them. At about 0400 on August 10, Beser was finally able to get to bed.

By the end of the week, with the Russians in the war and the advent and release of the atomic bombs, it was just a matter of time and the speed with which the Japanese government could move before the war would be over. In the interim, the killing went on, as did preparations for the invasion of the empire. Japan was hanging on the line. The men of the 509th wouldn't say that their two missions ended the war, but they sure went a long way toward hastening the final curtain.

*   *   *

27

SUMITERU TANIGUCHI, SIXTEEN YEARS OLD

Sumiteru Taniguchi is famous. You've seen him in this book. He is the boy in the picture whose back was burned off by the flash of Fat Man, the bomb that detonated over Nagasaki. The picture can't show you, though, that he had to receive treatments and lie on his stomach for a year and nine months. One day toward the end of his hospital stay, he came down with a fever. For four days, his temperature didn't break. He thought it might finally be it for him. On the fifth day, Taniguchi smelled smoke. A nearby soldier was puffing away on a cigarette. The dying teen begged him for one, and the soldier, noticing his pitiful state, felt sorry for him and offered one up. Taniguchi smoked it, and miraculously, his fever broke. For some reason that medicine has never explained, cigarettes saved his life. He since smoked two packs a day until a few years ago, when he caught pneumonia one summer. He has had to cut back since then. Now he smokes only one pack a day. His son is a doctor and advises against it, but Taniguchi knows why his life was spared, and he doesn't think smoking will kill him. He believes he was saved to warn people about the atomic bomb. He is a physical testament of its indiscriminate power.

My mother died a year and a half before the bomb, and my father was working in Manchuria. My sister, my brothers, and I were taken to my mother's parents' house in Nagasaki, and like everyone else, we lived in poverty. Because of the poverty, my eldest sister had to go out and start working, and as soon as I graduated from school, I got a job at the post office. As a duty of post office workers, even though I was very young, I still had to sometimes work nights, even during the air raids. One of my senior colleagues asked me to take his nightshift on August 9. I was supposed to work that afternoon, but I was already working that morning shift, too. My grandma always used to pack a lunchbox for me, but because I had to work all day, I ate two bentos, for breakfast and lunch, and took off for my full day of work. I set out for the outskirts of the city, which is now Nagasaki City, on my way to work.

On that morning, the air-raid alarm was on again, so I had to take temporary shelter at a small post office that was two kilometers away from the hypocenter near Tsumibashi. A little while later, the alert was lifted, so I took off on my bicycle. I heard the roar of an airplane and thought it was strange because the alarm had been turned off. I tried to look back, and at that moment, I saw the enormous flash and was blown away. The heat, as I would learn later, was between 3,000 to 4,000 degrees Celsius. I was blown across the road and had to try to stick to it because the blasts kept coming. I remember the fear that I might die on that spot, but I encouraged myself not to die like this. I also remember looking around and seeing that almost all of the houses had totally collapsed. Only the house where I had last delivered my post was still standing, for some reason. I was blown, along with my bike, four meters.

When I came to my senses, I realized the skin on my left arm was hanging down, burned, and all of my clothes were crisped to almost nothing. I found my bike was bent severely. Even though I knew I was burned, I didn't feel any pain, and I wasn't bleeding.

I didn't feel any pain, but I still remember the tragic sights unfolding around me. I remember thinking, *Where can I get relief?*

I remember seeing two children lying dead, one totally black, the other without any signs of physical wounds. *How can he be dead if he wasn't injured?* I wondered, knowing nothing about radiation at the time.

My back and my left arm were severely burned, and my pants were basically burned. But a part of my right arm was saved from the burns, and the lower half of my body was saved. I knew there had to be a safe place, so I started look-ing for one. I found a tunnel operated by a weapons facility that I thought must be safe. There were some people giving any medical care that they could in the tunnel, and I had them cut off the hanging skin from my fingertips and arm.

People feared a second bombing, and we had to be transferred. When I tried to stand up, I didn't have any strength and couldn't move. Some people kindly carried me to a hillside, where I saw so many people dying and asking for water without anyone being able to help them. All of the hibakusha saw people asking for water; I think the burns made them even more dehydrated. We had to stay overnight on the hillside. The city of Nagasaki was on fire, everywhere, and we just watched helplessly. I saw one plane flying low over the city, still trying to make us suffer even after the bombing. Even at two o'clock in the morning, some people started walking toward the railway, and many died along the way.

The next day, many people left the hillside, but I had to stay there at least one more night before I could move without much help. Finally, on the third day, a rescue group reached us and took us to Isihaya, about twenty kilometers away. The hospital had already filled up, so they took us to the elementary school, where I remember lying on the floor.

Even though I had been taken by the rescue team, there wasn't any medication left to cure people, and people died all around me. For some reason, I didn't; I stayed alive. On the third day at the elementary school, I finally started bleeding, yet I didn't feel much pain. I was transferred to another place, but that doesn't mean there was more medication or sufficient care.

On September 8, I was transferred to another school, which had been turned into a hospital, in Nagasaki City, and finally, there was some medicine the doctors could use to heal my wounds. One procedure they could do was a blood transfusion, but it was hard for them to put blood in my veins.

I was only skin and bones, and the doctors suggested I eat raw cow liver to produce more blood, but it didn't help. Under those circumstances, people were dying one after another, and I assumed I would be next, but my time never came. The Americans provided us with penicillin.

For the next year and nine months, I was unable to move, and I lay on my stomach. In May of 1947, I finally became able to sit up. On March 20, 1949, I left the hospital in Omura and returned to Nagasaki. My wounds had not healed completely, so I had to be treated in Nagasaki. Even after fifteen years, my wounds did not heal.

During that time, I was in pain. I suffered, and I wanted to die. I finally asked for a week's leave from work and left home without telling anyone. I went to Karatsu in the Shiga Prefecture to die. I climbed the hills and went to the sea to think about it.

I thought about all the people who died. Although I was in pain, I was still alive. When I thought about who did this crime to me, I realized that I must live on behalf of those who died unwillingly. I had to tell what happened, so they did not die in vain.

Still, the physical pain persisted. Sometimes I visited two or three hospitals a day in the hope that they could heal my wounds.

My wounds weren't properly treated until 1960. That was fifteen years later. It wasn't easy. Then, I developed a tumor where the skin had burnt, and the doctor told me it was cancer. The war ended years ago, but not for us. We victims have been suffering every day since.[2]

*   *   *

---

2   The detail about his tumor comes from an interview with PBS. See Works Cited.

28

THE HEART IS MINDFUL

1985

"Do you feel any remorse?" asked Steve, nearly done with the interview.

"No. No," Jake repeated firmly. "I, as an American serviceman, was doing what was asked of me. I had the opportunity to back out. I didn't *have* to go. To get into the cutting edge of new technology, any engineer would have given their eye to get a role in it. Some people took it badly, like Oppenheimer." Jake looked down. "Yeah, he was upset, but I don't feel that way."

"How *do* you feel?" pressed Steve further, digging for a human reaction.

"Well, you can almost rationalize your feelings any way you want. I never give it a second thought until once a year the media comes around and starts asking me questions."

Steve pressed further. "I have met one woman who lives in Hiroshima already. She's a teacher. She's concerned about world peace. What do you do? Are you concer—"

"Concerned about it?" interrupted the growingly frustrated veteran. "Of course I'm concerned about it! I'm a parent. I'm a grandparent. I'm a human being. War isn't fun. I go out and talk to a lot of people: universities, high schools, whoever will have me. I don't hold back. The message is clear."

Not to Steve, it wasn't. So he asked, "What's the message?"

The Hiroshima heat weighed on Jake harder than the answers that were swimming in his head. "We have an obligation to rebuild the world we live in and to make sure another nuclear weapons attack is not possible. It's that simple. The governments are responsible. If half the people couldn't care less, their politicians won't do anything. If they express themselves, they'll do something about it."

"So your message is, make your thoughts known?" asked Steve, dissatisfied.

"It's not an easy thing to do. As time goes on, those of us who were a part of all this won't be around. As long as we have our health and our minds, we have to work and do something."

"A Japanese writer said this," Steve offered. "He said it was 'the worst sin committed in the twentieth century.' He called it the worst sin of the century. What's your reaction?"

"To each his own," said Jake quickly. "If you were a giver, you had one reaction. If I were on the receiving end, I might feel the same way. I can't disagree with him. I wasn't here blown off my feet and burned, maimed as so many of these people were. I think that's a perfectly natural reaction, and I have no disagreement with him. He's stabbing at the conscience of the world; unfortunately, he's stabbing at the Americans for what they did. I wouldn't say it was our proudest moment. I don't think any act of war is a proud moment. You take the terrible tragedies of the fire bombings in World War II; this was peanuts. Look at Osaka, Tokyo, Nagoya, Frankfurt, and Dresden. Sixty million people were killed over that time period. That's a lot of wasted lives. Are we going to do that again?"

"Do you think what you're doing is paying back?" pressed the diligent reporter.

"No. This isn't paying back. We don't do that," said Jake steadfastly. "What it hopefully will do is make sure it doesn't happen again. You can't pay back. You can't do that for the family who lost that person. We could never pay them back. I think it's important that people understand that this wasn't just a circus act we pulled off. It wasn't a one-time thing. Every day, we live under the nuclear threat. As long as that exists, we're all in trouble. When I look at my grandchildren, and they get to be twenty-one or twenty-four, like I was forty years ago, they don't have to go through what I did. We had children die in World War II for a lot less reason than the Japanese sure did. Somehow we must understand that there must be a better way. We gotta find it."

*　*　*

At 10:00 a.m., the crew took a "cool off" break from the boiling humidity. By this time, Michiko had returned with Miss Tazu Shibama, an eighty-year-old English teacher who had agreed to meet the American lieutenant. Shibama-san was no more than four feet tall. She wore a traditional tan kimono with a matching tan obi belt and a navy-blue mesh snood. She was frail-looking but was animated and effervescent in demeanor. Although she was missing a few teeth, which made understanding her slightly difficult, she chose her words carefully, and her English was poetic. The crewman and a survivor of his mission met in front of the Children's Peace Monument. They grasped each other's hands.

She told the crewman the story of Sadako Sasaki, "the little girl who was suffering from leukemia at age twelve. She tried to fold one thousand paper cranes to grant her wish of survival, but she passed away. Now every year, thousands of children bring strings of one thousand paper cranes to adorn her monument, wishing that no more survivors die from the bomb's effects."

As the sun rose over the open monument, the pair found a nearby park bench in the shade where they could comfortably talk.

"At eight o'clock, I sat down to eat my breakfast," she recounted, "because at eight thirty, I would have to leave for work. At eight fifteen, there was an explosion, and my house fell down on top of me. I was buried in the debris. My neighbor, who was blown over to my house, began to look for me, and he pulled me out from under the debris. I was not hurt, only very dusty and shook up. It was a miracle."

"I would say you are very lucky, looking at you. Did you get hurt at all?"

"No, none of my bones were broken," she said gratefully.

"You were extremely fortunate," he said.

"I know." She smiled.

"I saw people at the hospital yesterday with one arm or one leg. It's the tragedies of war they live with. I can't help but admire the people in this city, having lived through all of this. It's tremendous."

"All of my friends like the American way. After the occupation, soldiers came over to Japan. Those soldiers were very kind to Hiroshima people."

"I spoke to friends of *mine* who were in the occupation here. They were pleasantly received and surprised to see the Japanese didn't think they were monsters, hating them because of the beating you took. There's no way around it. I mean, because of Pearl Harbor, and—"

"Of course, *we* had nothing to do with all of that," she said. "Only the militarists and authorities planned these things. Tokyo wanted this."

"That's right," he said.

"It was just that the situation was wartime," she contin-ued, "nobody could use their common sense." She spoke with sincerity.

"What would you like me to tell the Americans?" asked Jake.

"Please tell your American friends that education is the most important thing." Her voice was calm yet certain. "Our children should be taught to love and work together as friends. That is the way we make this world a very happy place to live."

"That's almost the same message I brought with me," Jake said excitedly. "We come from different parts of the world with a common idea, and that's what it's going to take. It's going to take a lot of education. That's why I came, to educate myself. To see what Japan was like today versus how it was in World War II. Just these few moments with you have made this entire trip worthwhile. You're a wonderful, wonderful woman."

"You, too. You are a wonderful man. I'm glad you have my idea in your head."

"From worlds apart, we share these common views," said Jake in amazement. "People are people, wherever they are."

Shibama-san smiled a wide, reassuring smile and said, "The heart is mindful."

*   *   *

29

A NUCLEAR FAMILY

2011

I said good-bye to Yuji and Masahiro in Nagasaki. After a life-changing trip with the families of Sadako Sasaki and President Harry S. Truman, I was off on my own in Japan. I first stopped in Osaka to spend the day with Mei and her family, to greet them a year after they sent me on this journey of understanding. They were pleased to be left out of the peace activities I was publicly engaging in with the Sasakis, though they commended me for them.

The next day, I set off for Tohoku, my favorite part of Japan, and the part that needed the most help, over a year after the crippling tsunami people were starting to forget. I took the shinkansen bullet train to Morioka, met my best friend in Japan, Tomo, and drove back to his hometown Ofunato. It was greener now, and much cleaner. There used to be a ship stuck a mile inland in front of people's houses. It was gone. The downtown area that had been reduced to debris fields was cleared away, replaced with temporary trailer shops.

Tomo brought me to the restaurant where our crew of volunteer bus drivers had all gathered. Wada-san, one of my favorite of the group, turned to another man I didn't know to explain, "Ari no Ojii-san (Ari's grandfather)," and I didn't need to hear the rest. I was nervous that he even knew about my connection to the atomic bombs. Tomohiro leaned over to me and whispered, "We all saw you on TV."

When I came to Ofunato a year before, and be-friended these people I only told a few of the volunteers why I was originally in Japan, and no one from the local community. I wanted to keep these two parts of my life separate. I didn't want it to interfere with their recovery. But after Wada-san's explanation, I was accepted into the group. If someone disagreed with my being there, it wasn't made known.

Another friend around my age I'll leave nameless sat next to me at the dinner table. As we ate and drank, he asked me point blank if I would write about Ofunato in my book. "I thought about it," I said. "Do you think it would be all right?" That's when he blurted out what I assumed was his answer, or maybe a misunderstanding of my question, "My father died. He was a postal work-er in Rikuzentakata, the city next door. He was swept away, But I'm not angry," he insisted. "The tsunami

was natural, and it happened to everyone. Yes Ari please
write about us."

Later I found out, his father's body was recovered 12
miles down the coast, and that he was considered lucky
because they at least recoverd the body.

To the Japanese, the Sanriku coast evokes qualities of the Pacific Northeast the way Americans associate the Puget Sound with the Pacific Northwest. Azure-blue waters crash along fjord-laden shorelines, forming peaceful inlet harbors. The local people speak a pecular Japanese dialect and live in quaint towns connected by the famous Sanriku railway. The iconic train ran up the whole coast until it was ripped apart by the Great East Japan Earthquake on March 11, 2011. As everyone as far as China grappled to understand the magnitude of the earthquake that was just felt, a wave swelled to ninety feet in Ofunato and crashed into the Tohoku coast. In Ofunato, people they say there were up to three tsunami waves.

I was told a story that the woman responsible for giving the tsunami warnings in Ofunato (virtually every settlement in Japan has a series of loudspeakers throughout the area to deliver tsunami and earthquake warnings) gave up her life to deliver her message to others. Apparently, she was still telling people to get to high ground when the waves crashed through her station.

Rikuzentakata, a twenty-minute drive from Ofunato with multiple waterfronts, was estimated to be 80 percent destroyed. Thousands along the coast were swept to sea or killed in the massive array of houses, cars, lampposts, and all that swirled into the tide.

When the disaster's true impact unfolded in the coming weeks, Ofunato was far from the radiation of Fukushima Dai-Ichi, but also far from the attention of the world. For precisely this reason, All Hands Volunteers, a disaster-relief organization, decided to open up shop to help clean up what they could.

Shinpei, the filmmaker who introduced me to the Sasaki family, was also a former volunteer with the disaster relief group. Some of his volunteer friends came to the screening of his latest film, and he invited me to speak. One couple approached me afterward to introduce themselves. "Have you ever thought about volunteering?" they asked. "It would be really helpful for you and your mission," said the wife frankly but hearteningly.

By the next week, I was on a bus to Ofunato. Nearly six months after the tsunami destroyed most of the Tohoku coast, it was still regarded a disaster zone, and you still couldn't reach it by train.

*   *   *

For the past few days, I had been outside in the rain, digging out the highway gutters—and loving every minute of it. The antidote to a month of thought devouted to atomic destruction and the mental stress it brought, was digging. The tsunami mud clogged the rain gutters on the sides of the roads. They flooded after every rainfall until All Hands Volunteers cleaned them out. They dug through over seven kilometers of the Akasaki highway by the time I arrived. I was only there a week, and I wanted to try another project All Hands was working on in Ofunato and Rikuzentakata.

All Hands had two sleeping options for their project in Ofunato. You could stay at the Fukushinosato (FS) center up on the hill. It was a nice facility, with indoor bathrooms and a nice sleeping quarter. You couldn't drink alcohol inside, and there was a building curfew of 10:00 p.m. Most people liked staying at Sakari much better. There was no curfew, and you could drink in the common area downstairs.

The Sakari neighborhood is centrally located in the heart of Ofunato. FS was on a hill in the outskirts, a thirty-minute walk from Sakari. I stayed there.

The energy in Sakari Base was palpable. The base itself used to be a gutted- out electronics store, but it now had a makeshift roof. All Hands made a deal in order to get it: they could stay there, but by the end of the project, they had to put a permanent roof on it. The main meeting room had a giant, twelve-rug tatami mat in the center, and one had to remove his or her shoes before stepping on it. Volunteers ate their meals there, and the meetings were held there after dinner. That night, when everyone picked their job assignments, I decided

I would try one of the more outside-the-box projects: photo cleaning.

I woke up the next morning and sauntered downstairs to the tatami mat to sip my morning coffee and check my e-mail. I received a message from my grant holders for the research of this book, perking me up a bit. It was a response to my last update informing them about my unusual detour to understanding Hiroshima and Nagasaki.

Having been looking for a way to give to the relief efforts themselves, they offered me a chance to extend my volunteering time by at least a month or more if I wanted. They would pay to extend my flight or buy me a new one if needed. After two days of digging out the highway gutters, I looked down at my blistered hands and around the base and saw dirty, fulfilled workers going to spend a day in the service of someone who needed it more than anyone who came here. I knew my airfare was locked in, and I could either use it or throw it away and just stay and waste $800. I had to keep the time extension undecided until I had the time to think, but I had to get started on my day's work.

As a photographer, I had a deep appreciation for the work being done to restore photographs. There were three photo operations taking place at All Hands. In Rikuzentakata, an offsite storage facility housed any and all salvageable items, including thousands of photo albums. Satoko Kono had already attempted to physicaly wash hundreds of photos that had been found in town and handed in. She had studied paper conservation in London. She taught Becci, a photo retoucher and her original team how to wash photos.

People heard that All Hands was washing recovered photos and started bringing their own waterlogged albums to Sakari Base. Becci looked at some of the more precious moments and knew that she could fix some of them digitally. She also knew other artists who could fix them too. Photo retouchers tend to be savvy when it comes to digital communication. Before long, over five hundred digital retouchers around the world were working on cleaning photographs. Ninety families had hundreds of photographs restored to perfection. Her teams on two bases hand-washed well over one hundred thousand damaged and waterlogged photographs. They were displayed at a warehouse in whatever condition we could get them that was at least sanitzied. People could come and sift through and by the end of the project we had returned at least half of the salvaged items.

My team for the day, Kim 1 and Erica, converted the usual dining area into our washing station. We spread the waterproof tablecloth and filled up giant vats with cold water. Becci came over with the day's box of damaged photographs that been sitting in stacks for five months after being inundated with tsunami water. We washed a vat of baseball pictures that had been glued together after months of drying in a pack. Becci and her partner "Tree," the project director, taught me how to wash a picture.

First, wearing latex rubber gloves, you submerged a single photograph in clean, cold water. You rubbed the edges of the picture, removing excess mud and dirt, and then lightly brushed the image. Depending on the damage the picture had sustained, it either cleaned nicely or deteriorated in the water. It couldn't always be done, but if you could, it was crucial to at least save a face. You didn't know if that face was still alive or if it was the last picture of that person.

That day, I was working with Kim and Erica. They called her Kim 1 because there were two. Apparently, they were up their thirteenth Chris by my arrival. Kim 1 was a few years older than I. She told us she was an English teacher in Gifu Prefecture. She must have already known Erica by then because she asked only me why I was in Japan. I said to both of them, "Well, I"—*How much should I admit?*—"came here because my granddad was on the planes that dropped the atomic bombs."

This surprised Erica and Kim 1. Kim didn't reveal much but said, "Your grandfather saved my grandfather's life."

This caught *me* off guard.

"My grandfather's boat had arrived in Japan, and his unit was scheduled to go into battle the day after the first bomb was dropped. It was cancelled due to the bomb. I've always felt hesitant to criticize its dropping because he was *that* close. I don't know if I would have felt the same if he was just sailing over. All I know is that if he didn't survive, I wouldn't be here."

"Neither would I," chimed in Erica, who was mindlessly putting a stack of photos into an empty photo album while our Japanese volunteer did the same. "I forget exactly what he did, but my grandfather was involved in the Hiroshima mission, too. He was on one of the weather planes. We think he was a photographer because we have all of the pictures he took, like pictures of the mushroom cloud."

"Maybe our grandfathers knew each other!" I laughed.

I smiled, and we went back to washing pictures, thinking of all the serendipitous connections that led me to Ofunato and deeper into my understanding of the atomic bomb. Shinpei connected me to All Hands and Sadako Legacy. One person at a time, I learned something. I picked up a single picture left in the box. It was bigger than the rest, an 8x10 group shot. I looked closer and realized it was an old Japanese troop reunion on Saipan. I had seen countless photographs of my grandfather's own reunions. I hung it to dry and made up my mind. I wasn't going to throw away my plane ticket. I would go home. It cost the same to buy another plane ticket as it did to change it. I wanted to go home, anyway. So I did. But I wouldn't stay long.

They grant agency agreed and bought me a one-way ticket back to Japan fifteen days after my departure. My last night, Shinpei called me and surprised me by saying, "I've been driving down the Tohoku Coast, just getting a scale for the disaster, collecting stuff for an art project, I think—still not sure yet. Anyway, I'll be passing through Ofunato tonight. Want to get dinner?"

Over tempura and beer, Shinpei revealed to me what he saw. "The coastline looks likes Hiroshima and Nagasaki all the way down. It's Unimaginable."

The following day, I left Ofunato. Eight hours later, I had returned to my apartment, rented for the month in West Japan. The next day, I flew from Osaka to Finland, Finland to New York, New York to Baltimore. I spent ten days in the discomfort of my home, where nothing had changed and the world hadn't ended. I knew where I needed to be.

I flew to Los Angeles, stayed a day with my friend and flew to Tokyo. Fifteen days after leaving project, I was back full circle around the world. I was still in the middle of a journey that has yet to really end, even as I write these words four years later. I believed once that if I didn't give up, I would continue to meet people who would only deepen my understanding and further me along this path. I wasn't prepared for what would happen over the next two months.

My bus turned the corner, and I woke up from my first-ever sleep on a night bus. The whole of what used to be Rikuzentakata formed into view as the sun began to rise over the coastline. Had Fukushima not faced melt down, the world would have known Rikuzentakata as the symbol of the tsunami. The lone, eighty-eight-foot-tall "miracle pine tree" that endured the tsunami where seventy thousand once stood was there. Nearly empty of pine leaves, except for a tuft at the top where the waters didn't reach, it had withered to skeletal remains. It has become Tohoku's symbol of resilience in the face of disaster, its own kind of atomic-bomb dome.

Months later, I ignorantly described the view as disheartening to a fellow volunteer. "To see what was once city turned into piles and fields was devastating," I said to him earnestly.

This particular volunteer had arrived in Japan two weeks after the tsunami had hit. He was the first volunteer, and he arrived in Ofunato by accident, but that's a different story. He worked for three months, his visa ran out, and so did his money. He went home, worked his way back, and returned to project while I was returning home for my break. When met later, I told him of my disappointment, he shook his head and said, "When I saw all the fields on my bus ride back in, I was excited! You should have seen what those fields looked like six months ago. They've worked so hard! And so quickly to clean it up!"

What was left of the debris of Rikuzentakata disappeared out of view as the bus drove through a tunnel about ten minutes away from its next stop. My stop. Ofunato. As had become my habit, I pulled out my iPhone and started typing a fresh note that I thought was supposed to begin my book.

Everyone I met along this journey is working to make the world better than the way they found it. Some

people I've met want to rid the world of nuclear weapons. Some people I've met want to reconcile with their former enemy. Some people just want to do work for someone in need. Some people just want to get by.

On August 6 and August 9, America dropped two atomic bombs on top of five hundred thousand people in Hiroshima and Nagasaki, killing two hundred thousand of them. Sixty-six years later, a tsunami washed away almost twenty thousand people and sent the Fukushima Dai-Ichi Nuclear Plant into a core meltdown, displacing nearly three hundred fifty thousand and creating a twelve-mile-radius exclusion zone of radioactive wasteland. Only in Japan.

Everyone has his or her own cause. Everyone has his or her own reason for coming to volunteer. You just have to figure out who it is you're fighting for, writing for, or building for. There is something that connected me to the people in this book, the people who taught me the lessons about the atomic bomb. We come from different countries, we think with different minds, and we even make our own kind of mistakes, but we work together like a family— a nuclear family.

* * *

Acknowledgments

To thank anyone who let me share his or her testimony seems wrong. I can't thank someone for living through something so horrible and bearing the weight to make sure it doesn't happen again. Yet, they have bravely allowed me to interview them and faced social stigma for speaking out. They want nothing more than to rid the world of these weapons, the weapons that have scarred the rest of their lives.

I'd like to thank the Asahi Shimbun for connecting me to Shinpei Takeda, who in turn I'd like to thank for connecting me to the family of Sadako Sasaki. Without your ambition to teach me the Japanese Perspective, Shinpei, I never would have come close to finishing this book. I want to thank the translators and coordinators in Japan who made these interviews possible: Tomoko Watanabe from Hiroshima ANT and Keiko Ogura, Tomoko Kakeda, and Kanade Kurozumi with Hiroshima Interpreters for Peace.

I want to thank Tomoko Maekawa, Takahashi Junpei, Yoshida Mutsuko, Masako Unezaki, and Ayumi Nakada for translating in Nagasaki. I also want to thank Yuji, Megumi, and Masahiro Sasaki; Masaki Kobayashi; and Kazuko Minamoto with Sadako Legacy. I want to thank Clifton Daniel, Kathleen Sullivan, Robert Croonquist, and Marie Cochrane with Hibakusha Stories for introducing me to so many amazing people who appear in this book and guiding me along this journey immeasurably. I want to thank Akira Kawasaki, Meri Joyce, Rika Watanabe, Saori Koga, and Mayu Seto for trusting me to work with you on Peace Boat, along with *all* of the communication coordinators, as well as Aiko Ichizuka, Ai Ito Onodera, Yoko Takayama, Sumiko Hatakayama, and Lisa Fang, who translated for the Hibakusha Project. I want to thank Ranko Fukuda for her beautiful translations of Kawamoto-san's interview. Becci, you taught me that discipline and hard work pay off and I carried that spirt in the writing of this book. Brett, you might have read this more than I have and deserve more than an editing credit.

To those who donated to my book through my GoFundMe campaign, you made this possible. This book is *our* accomplishment.

Thank you:

Walter Enloe
Aaron Kokubo Dean
Grace Ritchey
Nicholas Corsaniti
Sara Sherman
Ben Fitterman
Kenzie Rosen-Stone
Emily Kleinman
Kristopher Thornsbury
Abby Widom

Cynthia Hirsch
Jean Fedder
Andrew Cohen
The extended Beser family
The Baltimore Chavura
Zoe Morrison
Annabelle Kinney
Caroline Kinney
Terue Okada
Anonymous

WORKS CITED

WRITTEN SOURCES

Beser, J. *Hiroshima & Nagasaki: Revisited*. Memphis: Global Press, 1988.

Geddie, Bill, producer. *Good Morning America*. New York: ABC, August 6, 1985.

Interview with each hibakusha, oral histories of Jacob and Rose, interview with Eric Beser.
The A-bomb That I Experienced. Keijiro Matsushima. http://homepage2.nifty.com/wfchiroshima/ hibakushapdf/6MatsushimaStoryE.pdf

INTERVIEWS

Beser, Jacob. Personal communication. 1980, 1985.
Spangler, Jack. Personal communication. 2012.
Goto, Hiroyuki. Personal communication. 2012, 2013.

Kawamoto, Shoso. Personal communication. 2013.

Lee, Jong Keun. Personal communication. 2013.

Matsushima, Keijiro. Personal communication. 2011, 2012, 2013.

Nakamoto, Hatsuno. Personal communication. 2012, 2013.

Ogura, Keiko. Personal communication. 2011, 2012, 2013.

Sasaki, Masahiro. Personal communication. 2012, 2013.

Sasamori, Shigeko. Personal communication. 2015.

Shimohira, Sakue. Personal communication. 2013.

Tanaka, Toshiko. Personal communication. 2013.

Taniguchi, Sumiteru. *People's Century: Fallout.* PBS, June 15, 1999.

Taniguchi, Sumiteru. Personal communication. 2012, 2013.

Yahata, Teruko. Personal communication. 2013.

Yamazaki, Toshiko. Personal communication. 2013.

Made in the USA
Middletown, DE
30 July 2015